Friedrich Weinbrenner

Architect of Karlsruhe

Friedrich Weinbrenner
Architect of Karlsruhe

A Catalogue of the
Drawings in the
Architectural Archives of the
University of Pennsylvania

David B. Brownlee
Editor

UNIVERSITY OF PENNSYLVANIA PRESS
PHILADELPHIA   1986

upp

On the occasion of the exhibition

"FRIEDRICH WEINBRENNER, ARCHITECT OF
 KARLSRUHE"

Arthur Ross Gallery, University of Pennsylvania,
 Philadelphia
Stadtgeschichte im Prinz-Max-Palais, Karlsruhe
Busch-Reisinger Museum, Harvard University,
 Cambridge, Massachusetts
Art Institute of Chicago
The Octagon Museum, American Institute of Architects
 Foundation, Washington, D.C.
Canadian Centre for Architecture, Montreal

This exhibition was organized and the catalogue
prepared with the aid of a grant from the National
Endowment for the Arts.

This catalogue is published with the assistance of the
J. Paul Getty Trust.

Library of Congress Cataloging-in-Publication Data

Weinbrenner, Friedrich, 1766–1826.
  Friedrich Weinbrenner, architect of Karlsruhe.

  Bibliography: p.
  1. Weinbrenner, Friedrich, 1766–1826-Exhibitions.
2. Architectural drawing—19th century—Germany—
Exhibitions.   3. Karlsruhe (Germany)—Buildings,
structures, etc.—Exhibitions.   4. University of
Pennsylvania. Architectural Archives—Exhibitions.
I. Brownlee, David Bruce.   II. University of
Pennsylvania. Architectural Archives.   III. Arthur
Ross Gallery.   IV. Title.
NA2707.W45A4   1986   720'.22'2   86-7038

ISBN 0-8122-8010-5 (cloth)
ISBN 0-8122-1220-7 (paper)

Printed in the United States of America

Contents

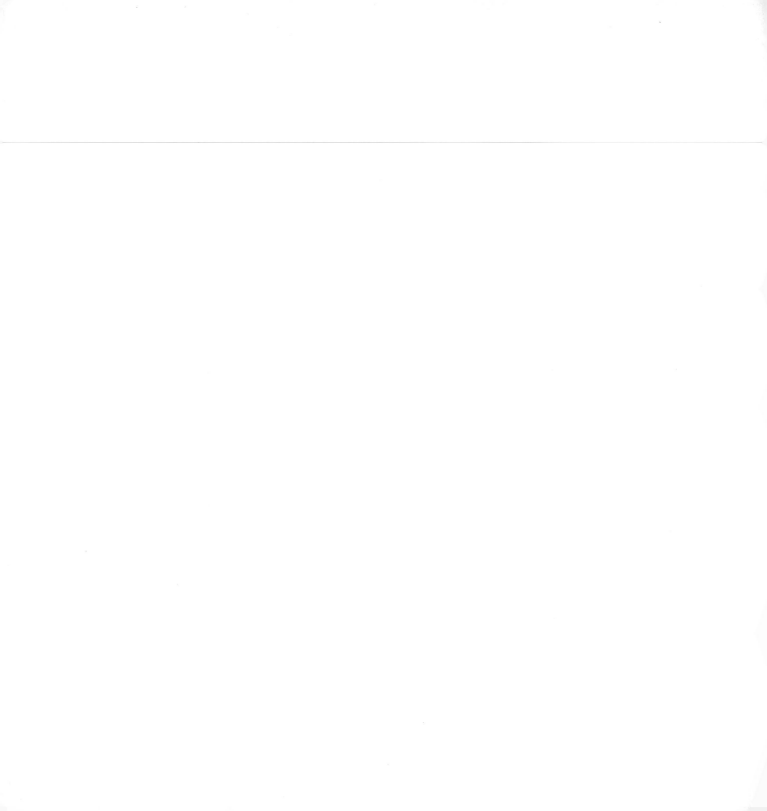

Preface and Acknowledgments

David B. Brownlee

FRIEDRICH Weinbrenner was the first important German architect of the nineteenth century. A transitional figure, he was born amid the free thinking of the Age of Reason, but he lived and worked in the materialist world of the modern era. Most of his architecture was built in Karlsruhe, the capital of Baden, in southwest Germany, and yet 281 of the most important drawings to record his work are in Philadelphia, in the Architectural Archives of the University of Pennsylvania. Although a few dozen of the drawings were published by Klaus Lankheit in 1976 and eleven traveled to Karlsruhe for display in 1977 and 1978, the collection has not before been systematically studied.

This volume is both a catalogue raisonné of the drawings and a record of their first major exhibition. Its structure has been decreed by the character of the collection. Introductory essays have been written and individual entries have been organized to reflect areas of special strength: Weinbrenner's buildings on the urban estates of the ruling family, his agricultural architecture, his town houses, an unusual selection of his public buildings, preparatory work for the illustrations of his *Architektonisches Lehrbuch*, and his heretofore almost unknown work as a decorative artist. No biography as such is offered, although the first essay does outline the major events of Weinbrenner's life.

Several of the essays have been prepared by or with the assistance of the art history graduate students enrolled in my Weinbrenner seminar in spring 1985: Leslie Blacksberg, Mark Crinson, Michael J. Lewis, Hollis Porter, and Robert Wojtowicz. They have also written most of the catalogue entries, as their initials show, and prepared the typologically related parts of the checklist. Uninitialed entries are the products of complex collaboration conducted under my guidance.

Our research has benefited hugely from the hospitality, support, and advice of many scholars and archivists in Karlsruhe. I offer my profound thanks to these colleagues and institutions: the Badisches Landesmuseum (Dr. Rosemarie Stratmann), Claudia Elbert, Gerhard Everke, the Generallandesarchiv, the Institut für Baugeschichte of the Universität Karlsruhe (Dr. Wulf Schirmer and Hanno Brockhoff), the Landesdenkmalamt (Dr. Hans Huth), the Staatliche Kunsthalle, and the Stadtarchiv (Dr. Heinz Schmitt).

The National Endowment for the Arts has generously supported this project, with additional funds having come from the Research Foundation of the University of Pennsylvania. Julia Moore Converse, Archivist of the Architectural Archives, has favored the Weinbrenner drawings with her diligence and energy, and, while preparing their exhibition, she has willingly shouldered much editorial responsibility. An abundance of archaic German script was deciphered by Martha Brantigan, Gabriele Gutkind, and Karen Purdy. Robert Wojtowicz has provided invaluable research and editorial assistance.

PHILADELPHIA,
SEPTEMBER 1985

Friedrich
Weinbrenner
Architect of Karlsruhe

Friedrich Weinbrenner and Karlsruhe: An Introduction

David B. Brownlee

FRIEDRICH Weinbrenner (1766–1826) was the son of a carpenter and a child of the Enlightenment.[1] During the decades in which the world plunged suddenly from ancien régime into modernity, he imprinted those two lines of filiation on his native Karlsruhe with an esthetic language that was at once practical and idealistic. Weinbrenner's art harnessed the infinite possibilities of the late eighteenth-century imagination to the infinitely complex business of nineteenth-century architecture.

Karlsruhe was the perfect arena for such labor. A product of the Enlightenment itself, the star-shaped city had been laid out in 1715 as a new capital—and a model of an orderly universe—for Margrave Karl Wilhelm, the ruler of the tiny southwest German state of Baden-Durlach (fig. 1). The margrave's successor was his grandson Karl Friedrich, whose marathon reign (1746–1811) saw the state through the revolutionary era. It was Karl Friedrich who negotiated the inheritance settlement that brought the margravate of Baden-Baden under his rule in 1770, doubling the size of his domain and its population. Then, after waging war unsuccessfully against the neighboring Republic of France in the 1790s, he accepted a policy of compulsory neutrality and, ultimately, the military alliance imposed by Imperial France. He profited accordingly. In 1803, together with further territorial annexation, he took the title elector, and in 1806, when Napoleon rationalized the borders of his German allies, he became the grand duke of a Baden that counted almost one million inhabitants, dwelling for the first time on wholly contiguous lands.

Karl Friedrich was a broadly educated and tolerant sovereign, and he and his extraordinary first wife, the "all-knowing and all-asking" Karoline Luise, enjoyed the confidence of many of the leading thinkers of eighteenth-century France. A modernist in his political and economic thinking, he permitted the growth of a mighty official bureaucracy to control his expanding, modern state. Its members led a long campaign for increased bourgeois power, triumphing with the establishment of a constitutional grand duchy in 1818. Baden became the model of constitutionalism in nineteenth-century Germany.

In the arts, however, Baden, like all Germany, lagged substantially behind France, Italy, and England. The young Weinbrenner could find no one in his native Karlsruhe to instruct him in the rudiments of architecture in the 1780s, and thus he took drawing lessons and studied mathematics and physics. His father, a master builder, also instructed him in the family trade, and it was as a builder that he first traveled to Switzerland in 1788. But he stayed there until 1790 to further his study of drawing and learn French, making friends who helped his later career (see cats. 23, 24). A confirmed autodidact and certain that he should become an architect, he then journeyed to Vienna to enroll in the Academy. Weinbrenner was particularly intrigued by Vincenz Fischer's lectures on the rendering of light and shadow, and this subject later figured large in his

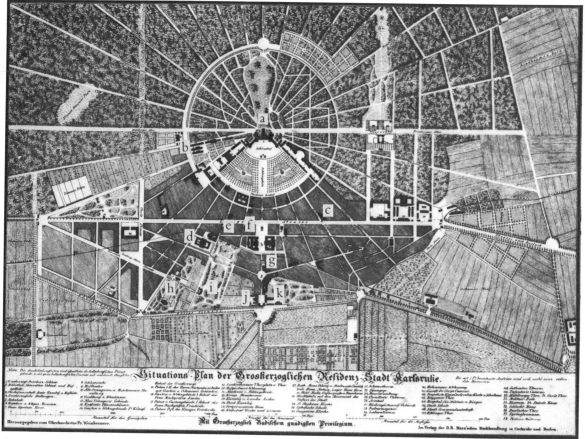

Fig. 1. Karlsruhe in 1822, with locations of buildings in the catalogue: *a* (cat. 15), *b* (cats. 60–67), *c* (cat. 50), *d* (cat 70), *e* (cats. 41–43), *f* (cat. 44), *g* (cat. 37), *h* (cats. 1–8), *i* (cats. 9, 10), *j* (cats. 35, 36), *k* (cats. 11–14). (*Stadtarchiv, XVI 11320*)

own *Architektonisches Lehrbuch* (cats. 73–79). Although delighted by its cosmopolitan and metropolitan character, he left the Austrian capital in fall 1791 and, finding little of interest in Dresden, reached Berlin by the end of the year.

In Berlin, where Weinbrenner learned much, he could see most of the recent developments of later eighteenth-century architecture in a microcosm. Palladianism, that antidote to the baroque and rococo styles that had swept through England in the second quarter of the century and reached France in the 1750s, had only found secure footing in Germany in the 1770s. But when Weinbrenner arrived in Berlin, Palladian taste was already being overlaid by the somewhat less tardy arrival of romantic neoclassicism, born in Rome around 1750. This complex situation is reflected in his *Denkwürdigkeiten*, which praise both the old-fashioned proto-Palladianism of Georg Wenzeslaus von Knobelsdorff's opera (1741–43) and the work of Hans Christian

Genelli, whose proposed monument for Frederick the Great had introduced the severe model of the Greek Doric temple to German architecture in 1787. Such respect for both conservative and innovative models shaped Weinbrenner's later work.

The curious omission of any mention of David and Friedrich Gilly in his autobiography does not mean that Weinbrenner was not also influenced by those most active and innovative Berliners. It was their informal and formal schooling that launched the first nineteenth-century generation of German architects, and the drawings in the Philadelphia collection demonstrate quite plainly that Weinbrenner was among them. To David Gilly he was indebted for the models for his later agricultural architecture (cat. 32). His earliest documented building, a thatched pavilion at Schackwitz (cat. 20), designed about 1794, bears comparison with Friedrich's contemporary work.[2] An even more profound influence is betrayed by Weinbrenner's ownership of one of Friedrich Gilly's sketches of medieval architecture; it places Weinbrenner close to the beginnings of the romantic and nationalist revival of German Gothic (cat. 84). Weinbrenner's reluctance to acknowledge this indebtedness in writing may be ascribed to the fact that Friedrich Gilly, already an inspector in the Prussian building department when they met in Berlin, was six years younger.

After little more than five months in Prussia, Weinbrenner went to Rome. During his five years in Italy he absorbed the lessons of neoclassicism and learned its established Roman models, but he also turned his attention to Greek architecture. He was one of the first German students to visit the temples built by Greek colonists at Paestum, and the blunt power of their early Doric gripped his imagination and colored many of his early projects (see cats. 57, 58). He sketched the vernacular of the Italian countryside and the urban architecture of the Renaissance as well; projects from the period show that he began to experiment with the Palladian forms he had discovered in Berlin, but he saw none of Palladio's buildings (cat. 80).

During his enormously extended student travels, Weinbrenner had begun to design buildings for Karlsruhe. This work grew out of the proposal for a new Marktplatz that he, like several senior architects, had prepared in 1790 and 1791 in response to an invitation from Karl Friedrich. The site lay south of the intersection of the Schloss Strasse (the city's north-south axis) and Lange Strasse (the great east-west street that had marked the southern boundary of the developed area). Weinbrenner's design of 1791 was for a rectangular forum, framed by a facing town hall and Protestant church. In Berlin in 1792 he began to flesh out this outline, preparing several schemes for a Pantheon-like church with an attached Doric portico; in Rome in 1794 he designed a blank-walled town hall in the laconic style of the French revolutionary classicists. With this preparation he was able to present a "General Bauplan" almost immediately upon his return to Karlsruhe in October 1797. This showed not only the Marktplatz with its church and town hall, but also the continuation of the Schloss Strasse southward through a circus, ending at a city gate on the road leading toward Ettlingen. His design bore with it the implication that all land south of Lange Strasse was to be developed.

Although Weinbrenner was entrusted with the design of a large synagogue in Karlsruhe in 1798 (cat. 50), he was frustrated by the conservatism of Bauinspektor Jeremias Müller, and he quit his native city again briefly from 1798 until 1800 to test the architectural waters in Hanover and Strassburg. But he soon returned to build a great Palladian palace for the three sons of Karl Friedrich's second wife, Luise Caroline, the Imperial Countess of Hochberg (fig. 2, cats. 11–14). Sited on the Rondellplatz, as the proposed circus was christened, this commission helped ensure the success of his proposed plan for the city as a whole, and the promising architect was thus encouraged to wait out the final months of Müller's life. In 1801 he succeeded to the post of *Bauinspektor* and built his own house on the Schloss Strasse next

Fig. 2. Margraves' palace on the Rondellplatz, c. 1936. (*Stadtarchiv, XIVa 267*)

to the Ettlingen Gate (cats. 35, 36).

Weinbrenner's control over the shape of Karlsruhe exceeded even that exerted by his contemporaries who built Washington, D.C., and remade Leningrad. As products of the same post-revolutionary era, the three cities evinced many of the same characteristics (see fig. 1). In each an armature of baroque avenues remained visible—in Karlsruhe as the inheritance from the plan of 1715—but the artistic emphasis had shifted from the contrivance of lengthy vistas to the control of urban space. Thus, while the central tower of Karlsruhe's Grand Ducal Palace, visible at the head of each radiating street, continued to express the ideals of earlier planning, it was counterpointed by the powerfully urban enclosures that Weinbrenner built in the Rondellplatz

and the Marktplatz. Each major street was also given an outer terminus, not in an obelisk or tower, but in a gate with its own encircled foreyard. By providing these alternative foci, Weinbrenner diminished the relative importance of the palace tower and gave expression to the ascendant power of the bourgeoisie.

It was the middle class who made Weinbrenner's practice of architecture possible and gave Karlsruhe its unusual atmosphere. The former carpentry apprentice appreciated bourgeois pragmatism and was able to translate the dreams of his Roman years into the wood and stucco architecture that his clients could afford to build. The urban imagery he created for Karlsruhe was accordingly bound up with the character of middle-class homes and institutions. No collection of individualistic palaces for the nobility could have defined the disciplined lineations of his plan so well, and only the churches and governmental buildings of the bourgeoisie provided him with the raison d'être for displacing the focus of the city from the Grand Ducal Palace to a forum south of the Lange Strasse. But while the energy of these clients was enormous, their resources were often constrained. Construction of the new Rathaus and new Protestant and Catholic churches began at about the time Baden became a grand duchy in 1806, but the work lagged during the Napoleonic Wars and none of the big buildings was completed before 1814.

While substantially occupied with this work for the citizenry of Karlsruhe, Weinbrenner naturally labored for the ruling family as well. Karl Friedrich had rebuilt the baroque palace before Weinbrenner even began to practice architecture, however, and in the last years before his death in 1811, the grand duke undertook little building save for Weinbrenner's court theater (1806–8), a conservative Palladian design, and the reconstruction of his country house at Bauschlott (cat. 30).

His children and his second wife were better clients. His eldest son from his first marriage, Crown Prince Karl Ludwig, engaged Weinbrenner to build a villa on his urban estate in the southwest quarter of the city, although he did not live to see its completion in 1802 (cats. 9, 10). Friedrich, his second son, did survive to see Weinbrenner's reconstruction of the castle at Neu-Eberstein between 1803 and 1804 (checklist 96.1–96.3) and his conversion of three smaller houses into one great urban palace in 1809 (see fig. 5, cat. 37). But the only new work he discussed with the architect, a villa on an estate adjoining Karl Ludwig's, was not built until after his death in 1817. This was a grandiose project, with a great Palladian house and numerous outbuildings set in an English-style garden (fig. 3, cats. 1–8). Weinbrenner's villas for the two brothers became the Karlsruhe residences of their widows, Amalie and Christiane Louise.

In Karl Friedrich's waning years, his second wife, a woman of ordinary birth who had been a member of his first wife's entourage, drew substantial power into her own hands. Luise Caroline showed special interest in the skills of the new *Baudirektor* and became one of his most important patrons. Having started him off with the commission for her sons' palace on the Rondellplatz, she asked him to design a model farm at Katharinental in 1808 (cats. 33, 34), an astonishing example of the advance of science into even the most traditional areas of human endeavor. Weinbrenner built for her at Rotenfels as well (cat. 18), and he further developed that property as a country seat for her son Wilhelm after 1818. When Karl Friedrich died Luise Caroline retired to the house that Weinbrenner had built for the grand duke at Bauschlott.

Because of the early death of his son Crown Prince Karl Ludwig, the passing of Karl Friedrich brought his grandson Karl to the throne in 1811. As Napoleon demanded, Karl had married the emperor's adopted daughter Stephanie in order to cement the alliance of Baden and France, and his brief rule (1811–18) began with a major rebuilding of the west wing of the palace for her use (cats. 60–67). After 1813 the Napoleonic defeat cast a pall over the household. Although Baden was allowed to preserve the great territorial annexations made under French protection, Karl never restored to the court the luster it had known in the best years of Karl Friedrich's long reign. Weinbrenner continued to frequent the much livelier circle that gathered around the widowed Luise Caroline. Her son Leopold ultimately succeeded to the throne because Karl and Stephanie could produce no male heirs, thus allowing the long-ruling Zähringer house to die out.

It is difficult to detect the effects of this cavalcade of bourgeois and princely life on Friedrich Weinbrenner. An amply built man, his stature was amplified and his position insulated by a large office and an enormous school—one of the first architectural schools in Germany—which he founded

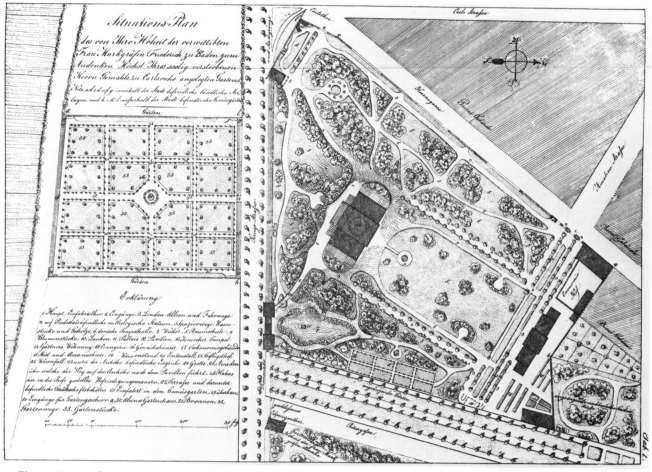

Fig. 3. Estate of Margravine Christiane Louise. (*Weinbrenner* [1822–35])

almost as soon as he returned permanently to Karlsruhe in 1800. His academy occupied rooms in his own home at the Ettlingen Gate, and he was always in the swirl of his work. Although he had spent five years in Italy debating architecture and philosophy with the leading intellects of his day, the endless routine of professional life robbed him of the time for such pursuits in Karlsruhe. When Goethe visited his city in 1815, the architect showed the visitor his new Catholic church (cat. 70) and museum and the greenhouses in the botanical garden (cat. 15).

He then spent several hours with a large party of admirers engaged in discussion with Germany's greatest man of letters. But Weinbrenner grew irritable, and Ferdinand Freiherr von Biedenfeld remembered him remarking crankily that

He would gladly spend a hundred years alone with Goethe; one savors thus the great mind of the man perfectly and learns something new from him every minute. But to chase after him like this in a crowd seems boring and almost like sycophancy.[3]

The architect soon slipped away, citing the press of official business.

Weinbrenner lived in and for his work, establishing the model for the great architectural offices of the later nineteenth century. The distinction between his private and public practices and his school was not always clear. His students were regularly asked to copy their master's recent designs, as if they were his draftsmen, and the best of them were promoted to teaching positions and then moved on to posts within the state architectural department. His roll of alumni was most distinguished, including many of the leading architects of the next generation. Among them were Georg Moller of Darmstadt, Alexis de Chateauneuf of Hamburg, and his own great successor in Karlsruhe, Heinrich Hübsch. Even Friedrich von Gärtner, the great Münchner, passed through Karlsruhe.

The result of this type of practice is to be found in the confusion surrounding the records of its accomplishments. The majority of drawings that show buildings by Weinbrenner do not seem to be in his hand. Some were probably produced in his office, while others were made as student exercises. The drawings also have been widely dispersed by pupils and assistants who wished to preserve a record of their time with him. Two large sketchbooks, the work of Heinrich Geier and D. Schumacher,[4] are evidence of the respect in which his work was held, and between 1847 and 1858 a group of his students pooled their drawings to publish four fascicles of a *Sammlung von Grundplänen, entworfen durch Friedrich Weinbrenner.*

The collection of drawings that has come to the University of Pennsylvania reflects these patterns of practice. Although the vast majority of the sheets record Weinbrenner's works, only two were signed by him, another seems to bear his initials, and a fourth was later labeled as being from his pen.[5] There are, on the other hand, a large number of drawings signed by students. Friedrich Arnold (1786–1854), a rather conservative architect who never strayed far from Weinbrenner's style, signed six

drawings in the collection. Most of these are for his own buildings, and there are a number of unsigned drawings for his works as well.[6] There is even a house design signed by one of Arnold's students, and there are several unsigned drawings showing the works of his brother Christoph.[7] A handful of sheets bear other signatures or show the work of other architects, but the largest group of signed drawings, twenty-four in all, is the work of the Thierry family: Ferdinand (c. 1777–1833), his brother Wilhelm (1761–1823), and Wilhelm's son Karl (1796–1858).[8] It is evident from this that Weinbrenner's circle was large and that architectural talents and ideas were freely shared among its members in early nineteenth-century Karlsruhe. Moreover, the large number of Thierry drawings reflects the fact that it was they who assembled the Weinbrenner collection that came to America; the collection was bequeathed by Karl to Theodore Thierry (c. 1805–70), an emigrant architect.[9]

Despite its French-sounding name, the Thierry family was native to Baden. Ferdinand and Wilhelm Thierry were born in Bruchsal, not far from Karlsruhe, and both were trained as architects by Weinbrenner. Ferdinand, whose architectural reputation was larger than his brother's, entered Weinbrenner's school shortly after its establishment and was soon hired as a drawing instructor. In 1803 he passed the licensing examination and entered the service of the state building department. He held a series of posts in and around Konstanz in the southernmost part of Baden, where he erected a number of small, bluntly detailed churches. In 1820 he was called to Heidelberg, and he served there until his death. His brother Wilhelm trained as a painter in Mannheim and entered court service in 1794 in the Thuringian Duchy of Sachsen-Meiningen, where his son Karl was born. Wilhelm occasionally dabbled in architectural design, and in 1810, having resolved to devote himself more seriously to that art, he journeyed home to Baden to study with Weinbrenner. His schooling was brief, and in 1812 he returned to the Thuringian Forest to accept the position of *Baudirektor* in Rudolstadt. Ferdinand, too, was subsequently offered commissions in that region, and both brothers worked in the Heidecksburg, Rudolstadt's eighteenth-century palace. Wilhelm's son Karl also turned to architecture, pursuing his career in Karlsruhe. By 1825, a year before Weinbrenner's death, Karl had been appointed an instructor in the Karlsruhe architecture school, where he had apparently taken his training; he was promoted to the rank of professor in 1839 and taught there until retirement.

Unfortunately, most of the signatures on Thierry drawings in the collection do not include first names or initials, making precise assignment of the work difficult. Many of the drawings that are simply signed "Thierry," however, bear early dates and portray Karlsruhe buildings, making it likely that most of them were executed by Ferdinand rather than the much younger Karl or the Thuringia-based Wilhelm. But it was Karl who cared for the family collection of drawings and willed it to Theodore Thierry (apparently Ferdinand's son). Theodore had established himself by about 1833 in Philadelphia, where he worked in the office of the prominent neoclassical architect John Haviland.[10] The drawings arrived in Philadelphia on October 25, 1859.

The Thierry family provenance explains the special character of the drawings in Philadelphia. They include virtually all the Thierry autographs known to exist; moreover, they appear to have been selected for their usefulness in the New World. Nowhere else is there such a collection of Weinbrenner's agricultural buildings, and the selection of small urban houses is also unusually large. The other peculiar features of the collection—the large number of decorative studies for the Grand Ducal Palace and the preliminary designs for the *Lehrbuch*—cannot be ascribed to their American destination. But they might be explained by the particularly close relationship between Ferdinand Thierry and Weinbrenner, which gave the younger artist access to some of his master's most interesting work. Indeed, some of the Pennsylvania drawings could have been a special bequest from the great architect who made

Karlsruhe one of the first modern cities, for Ferdinand Thierry was at Friedrich Weinbrenner's bedside on the night he died.

NOTES

1. The essential source for Weinbrenner's life remains Valdenaire (1919 [2d ed., 1926]), very usefully supplemented by Staatliche Kunsthalle (1977), and the other recent literature cited in the bibliography.
2. Alste Oncken, *Friedrich Gilly, 1772–1800* (1935; reprint, Berlin: Gebrüder Mann, 1981), pl. 68c.
3. Quoted in Bentmann (1969, 14).
4. Schumacher album, Landesdenkmalamt, Karlsruhe. Geier sketchbook, last recorded in Max Läuger collection.
5. Signed: 6.6, 160.1; initialed (?): 120.1; labeled: 156.1.
6. Signed or initialed: 94.1, 94.2, 154.1, 162.1, 194.4, 194.5.
7. The student was C. Eichelkraut, who signed 74.1. C. Arnold's work: 70.1, 80.1, 162.1–162.6.
8. August Mossbrugger: 176.1. L. Fugergi: 130.1. Miessel: 32.1, 104.1. "Ж": 8.1. "F": 40.1. There are two plans of Hübsch's Polytechnical School: 150.1, 150.2. F. Thierry: 170.1. K. Thierry: 14.1, 14.2, 58.2–58.6, 60.1, 98.1, 178.1, 194.13. Thierry without first name or initial: 6.1, 6.2, 6.4, 12.1, 20.2, 30.1, 30.2, 46.1, 62.2, 92.1, 92.2, 100.1. For [Johann Anton] Ferdinand Thierry, see Ulrich Thieme, Felix Becher, et al. (eds.), *Allgemeines Lexikon der bildenden Künstler,* 37 vols. (Leipzig: Wilhelm Engelmann, E. A. Seemann, 1907–50), vol. 33, 33; Joseph Sauer, *Die kirchliche Kunst der ersten Hälfte des 19. Jahrhunderts in Baden* (Freiburg im Breisgau: Herder, 1933), 617–18; Generallandesarchiv, Karlsruhe, 76/7838, 390/1780, 422/3. For Wilhelm Adam Thierry, see *Bau- und Kunstdenkmäler Thüringens: Herzogthum Sachsen-Meiningen,* vol. 1, pt. 1, fasc. 24: *Amtgerichtsbezirk Meiningen (Die Stadt Meiningen und die Landorte)* (Jena: Gustav Fischer, 1909), 266; Heinrich Jacobi, "Wilhelm Thiery [sic] als homburger Hofzeichenmeister und Revolutionär," in *Festschrift Berthold Rein zum 75. Geburtstag: Forschungen zur schwarzburgischen Geschichte,* ed. Willy Flach (Jena: Verlag der Fromannschen Buchhandlung, Walter Biedermann, 1935), 142–64; Thieme, Becher, et al., op. cit., vol. 33, 34–35. For [Ludwig] Karl Thierry, see Generallandesarchiv, Karlsruhe, 206/934.

9. K. Thierry's will, enclosing receipt signed by T. Thierry and family tree: Generallandesarchiv, Karlsruhe, 270/Karlsruhe IV 8525. The date at which the drawings were acquired by the University of Pennsylvania has not been discovered. This account of the Thierry family is much indebted to research undertaken by Michael Lewis in Philadelphia and Karlsruhe.

10. The Letourneau House (checklist 244.1) may be the work of T. Thierry.

The Architecture of the Agricultural Revolution

David B. Brownlee

WHILE MUCH of Friedrich Weinbrenner's architectural energy was expended in urban Karlsruhe, he was also active in the countryside of Baden, where he built and improved farms. This was a promising area of endeavor for turn-of-the-century architects, for a rapidly growing population had made German agriculture stupendously profitable in the second half of the eighteenth century. Prices in the first decade after 1800 reached 210 percent of their level in the 1730s.[1] Such profits spawned the rural equivalent of the industrial revolution, bringing scientific farming methods and newly invented economic analysis into the still medieval countryside. The seminal works of a vast agricultural literature appeared in the 1750s, and the list of relevant titles had swelled to more than 6,000 by 1803.[2] The new scientific farm also demanded a new architectural vocabulary.

Baden's role in this great movement was charted by her sovereign. Margrave (later Grand Duke) Karl Friedrich devoted much energy during the early years of his long reign to implementing the most up-to-date analysis of agricultural economics.[3] He was an enthusiastic proponent of Physiocratic thinking, which posited agriculture as the sole economic activity capable of generating true wealth, and he shared his ideas during the 1760s and 1770s with Pierre-Samuel Du Pont de Nemours and Marquis Victor de Mirabeau, two of the principal followers of Physiocracy's founder, François Quesnay. Karl Friedrich was himself the author of a Physiocratic tract, his "Abrégé des principes de l'économie politique" (1772), and he introduced the Physiocratic "single tax" experimentally (and without notable success) in several villages within his domain. Serious botanical research was also carried out in the Karlsruhe Palace gardens under the patronage of his first wife, the polymath Karoline Luise. But certainly his most tangible contribution to the transformation of rural life was his edict of July 23, 1783, freeing forever the serfs of Baden from their feudal obligations. No other important German state followed Baden's example, a product of French liberal ideas, until the new century had begun.

Yet Baden provided a poor testing ground for Karl Friedrich's grandiose plans. Like most of Germany, Baden saw no significant enclosure of agricultural land—no creation of agricultural units of rational economic scale—until the second half of the nineteenth century. Moreover, aside from the narrow Rhine valley and the rolling upland east of Karlsruhe, the state possessed little good farmland in the eighteenth century, and most of the great territorial annexations of 1805 and 1806 comprised the hilly lands of the Black Forest. It is not surprising that the largest advances in agriculture were made elsewhere, especially in the fertile grainlands of North Germany. The first German agricultural society, the Thüringische Landwirtschaftsgesellschaft, was founded in 1762, whereas the Landwirtschaftliche Verein für das Grossherzogtum Baden was not established until 1819. The major agricultural journal, the *Annalen der niedersächsischen Landwirtschaft* (whose title changed regularly after its founding in 1799), was based in Celle and then in Berlin. It was well established long before Baden's own *Land-wirtschaftliche Wochenblatt* first appeared in 1820. Even neighboring Württemberg had an agricultural school by 1818, something not created in Baden.

Weinbrenner thus had a peculiarly defined mission as an agricultural architect, and he depended heavily on the examples established elsewhere. His largest debt was to David Gilly, whom he had encountered in Berlin in 1792 and whose practice included much work for the great landowners who were "colonizing" the hugely expanded Prussian farmlands. As early as 1770, Gilly had designed a rectangular farm complex as an examination exercise, with half-timbered buildings gathered around a courtyard.[4] Much of Weinbrenner's work in Baden was evidently modeled on this project. Gilly later gathered his ideas in a *Handbuch der Land-Bau-Kunst* (1797), which passed through nine editions by 1836. It was to this book that Albrecht Thaer, the greatest agricultural theorist of Weinbrenner's generation, referred the architectural questions posed by the readers of his *Grundsätze der rationellen Landwirthschaft* (1809–12).[5]

Weinbrenner, like all Germans interested in agricultural matters, was also indebted to English examples, for the new scientific agriculture had gained a head start in Britain, with its early enclosure movement.[6] Indeed, English literature dominated both the fields of agricultural science and agricultural architecture. Thaer's first important book was an *Einleitung zur Kenntnis der englischen Landwirtschaft* (1798–1804), and the first book cited by Gilly in his *Handbuch* was John Plaw's *Rural Architecture* (1794).[7] Weinbrenner himself advised architectural students to include England (and Germany) in their travels "chiefly for the sake of agricultural building and wood construction."[8]

Weinbrenner's association with agricultural architecture began early in his career. During his years in Switzerland (1788–90) he supervised the construction of several farm buildings, and upon establishing himself permanently in Karlsruhe in 1800 he was quickly employed in agricultural work.[9] He enjoyed the special favor of Luise Caroline, Karl Friedrich's second wife, and it was for her sons that he built the Margraves' Palace on the Rondellplatz (cats. 11–14), his first commission from the ruling family. It was also for her that he built his most complete model farm, Katharinental, in 1808 and 1809 (fig. 4, cats. 33, 34). A self-sufficient agricultural unit, its buildings lie alone in the center of a broad valley, unlike the surrounding farms, whose houses and barns line the main streets of nearby villages like Göbrichen. The rectangular plan was impressively rational, creating a virtual fertilizer factory overseen by the farmhouse at one end, and the placement of barns and living quarters in the very center of the worked lands was demonstrably efficient. Nevertheless, Katharinental was rarely emulated. Only the grand ducal household, for whom Weinbrenner also worked at Rotenfels and Bauschlott (cats. 18, 30), or a major capitalist like David Seligmann, for whom he built a farm closely modeled on Gilly's design of 1770 (cat. 32), could break the established landholding patterns.

Most of Weinbrenner's agricultural work was accordingly more piecemeal. There were numerous barns and small houses that could take their places within the familiar system of design and construction (cats. 28, 29, 31). It seems, in fact, that Weinbrenner, like Gilly, intentionally adopted half-timbering to show his respect for local conventions, as well as his admiration for wood construction. He also built a number of greenhouses (cats. 6, 16), and while some were frivolous in purpose, the utilitarian complex erected in the Karlsruhe botanical garden (cat. 15) served serious scientific ends.

Circumscribed as it was, this work was also erected on the insecure foundation of agricultural prosperity. The export price of German wheat peaked in 1801, and while southwest Germany was spared the first effects of the ensuing recession, the Napoleonic blockade of England (1806–13) wrought havoc with agriculture everywhere on the Continent.[10] There was a brief peacetime resurgence in 1814, but the imposition of import tariffs by the English Corn

Fig. 4. Katharinental from the south. (*D.B.*)

Law of 1815 caused a second collapse, and little was built in the next decade. The worst year of the crisis was 1825, the year before Weinbrenner's death.

NOTES

1. Wilhelm Abel, *Agricultural Fluctuations in Europe from the Thirteenth to the Twentieth Centuries*, trans. Olive Ordish from 3d German ed. (New York: St. Martin's Press, 1980), 198.

2. Wilhelm Abel, *Geschichte der deutschen Landwirtschaft vom frühen Mittelalter bis zum 19. Jahrhundert*, vol. 2, in Günther Franz, ed., *Deutsche Agrargeschichte* (Stuttgart: Eugen Ulmer, 1962), 257–66.

3. Markgräflich Badische Museen (1981), 216–19; Otto Moericke, *Die Agrarpolitik des Markgrafen Karl Friedrich von Baden* (Karlsruhe: Gottlieb Braun, 1905).

4. Marlies Lammert, *David Gilly, ein Baumeister des deutschen Klassizismus* (Berlin: Akademie-Verlag, 1964), 41–46.

5. Albrecht D. Thaer, *Principles of Agriculture*, 2 vols., trans. William Smith and C. W. Johnson (London: Ridgway, 1840), vol. 2, 761, 804.

6. John Martin Robinson, *Georgian Model Farms* (Oxford: Oxford University Press, 1983).

7. David Gilly, *Handbuch der Land-Bau-Kunst, vorzüglich in Rücksicht auf die Construction der Wohn- und Wirthschafts-Gebäude für angehende Cameral-Baumeister und Oeconomen*, 2 vols., 2d ed. (Berlin: Friedrich Vieweg, 1798), vol. 1, 1.

8. Weinbrenner (1810–25, vol. 1, fasc. 1, x).

9. Weinbrenner (1958, 24).

10. Abel, op. cit. (1980, 221–26).

Bourgeois Homes in a Liberal Setting

Mark Crinson

THE ARCHITECTURAL patterns for royal, patrician, and civil servant life were well established in Karlsruhe by the time Weinbrenner became *Baudirektor* in 1801. The finest houses were built closest to the center, where the Grand Ducal Palace's angled wings defined the breadth of growth within the radiating streets to the south. Appropriately, the nobility tended to live on the innermost ring of the plan, while the civil servants resided on the outer ring of the court circle.

The varieties of modern middle-class life and its architecture, however, were still unformed, pushed south of the Lange Strasse and given only a schematic armature by the radiating streets. Here was Weinbrenner's principal theater of activity. In the Marktplatz he created a subsidiary focus for middle-class institutions, and he also designed many of the town houses that filled in the surrounding streets, demarcating major arteries and public spaces and regulating the appearance of the whole. The result was a remarkably controlled architectural portrayal of an evolving social order.

While this urban environment was being built, Baden's constitutional reforms were redefining the relationship between the state and its citizens and creating the new and powerful groups that became Weinbrenner's clients. In most towns in Baden, the liberalization that promised the middle class unprecedented legal and administrative freedom also reshaped the bourgeoisie by challenging the strong social definitions of the traditional, guild-based burgher groups. Now in jeopardy were the codified

distinctions among protected, honorary, and full burghers; the system of vetting that admitted new members; and the sense that the community was an extended family led by the chief burghers.[1]

The first manifesto of this new liberalism was Johann Friedrich Brauer's "Hofratsinstruktion" (1794), in which he defined a constitution enshrined in the legal system that would limit the powers of the ruler. This text, which laid the intellectual groundwork, was followed by Brauer's seven constitutional edicts (1807–9), which bolstered the power of the central government in Karlsruhe and attempted to adjust the privileges of several social groups. The second of these edicts placed all towns under direct state (Baden) government, usurping the established power of the burghers. In the sixth edict the concept of state citizenship was inaugurated, guaranteeing rights to own property, pursue commerce and trade, establish a family, and enter the civil service. Citizenship was granted to the nobility, the burghers, and civil servants. Since most in these groups enjoyed such rights already, the edict's intent, like that of all seven, was above all to promote social cohesiveness under the central direction of Karlsruhe.[2] The transfer of power to the state bureaucracy was increased by the introduction of the Napoleonic code in 1809, and this process culminated in 1818 with the adoption of a state constitution.

These constitutional changes exaggerated the conditions that already existed in Karlsruhe, where traditional burghers had never possessed the power they enjoyed in smaller towns. This is most comprehensibly laid out in that period's social registers, in which the court is shown as the topmost tier of the Karlsruhe hierarchy, followed by numerous members of the civil service and the military, and finally by a fourth prestigious class of artists and professionals.[3] The leading role played elsewhere by the old bourgeoisie was not established in Karlsruhe because the newly created capital demanded the presence of the court and a bureaucracy that grew as the government became more centralized and the nation expanded. This process accelerated when the state quadrupled in size under Napoleon's protection.

In Karlsruhe unique social importance was attached to civil servants, on whom, along with the military, the city's prosperity depended, and the subsequent relative weakness of the burghers favored the aspirations of other groups as well. Professionals, who were unusually numerous in the capital, new groups of socially mobile entrepreneurs, and artists all worked in close alliance with the state. The greater number of Weinbrenner's town houses were designed for these still disenfranchised but ambitious bourgeois groups. Given their accord with the aims of the state, it was inevitable that they should award their own commissions to the state architect. Weinbrenner's influence on the outward complexion of the town was such that there was little other choice.

Most of the new town houses in the first two decades of the century were erected in the streets cutting east and west across the radial armature. The Zähringerstrasse, with a total of thirty-five houses built between 1804 and 1818, had by far the largest amount of construction in this period, followed by the Lange Strasse with twenty-four, and the Erbprinzenstrasse with sixteen.[4] The Zähringerstrasse developed rapidly; in 1780 no building existed on that street, which then only ran eastward from the Marktplatz. The first buildings were probably the garden houses erected in the early 1800s to serve the residences that lay to the north (cat. 21). With the replanning of the Marktplatz, the Zähringerstrasse

was driven westward as far as the Lammstrasse, and this western side, extended to the Ritterstrasse by 1823 and having acquired a kink in its course by 1834, was the most heavily developed in those decades.[5] The Sommerschuh house,[6] the house at number seventy-seven (see checklist 76.1),[7] and the earlier project for the Holb house (cat. 42), show that the Zähringerstrasse was notable for the individuality of its residences in an area otherwise filled with similar rowhouses.

The crests of building activity in the town occurred between 1810 and 1811 and between 1815 and 1818;[8] the latter peak was probably the result of the coinciding agricultural crisis in Baden, which accelerated migration to the towns. The urban transformation was most necessary and most extensive along the widest east-west street, the Lange Strasse, where there were a large number of odd-sized and decaying houses, and in and around the Marktplatz, the as yet unfocused hub of middle-class institutions.

Weinbrenner's role in all this was crucial, not only as an agent of architectural production, but also as an arbiter of the style and deployment of buildings throughout the town. His designs for model facades (dated 1804 and 1814–15) were intended to guide a controlled variety of detail and height. The 1804 design was the model for houses on the Marktplatz.[9] Four-story facades, including a mezzanine, were destined for its east and west sides adjacent to the Evangelische Stadtkirche and the Rathaus, and three-story facades for its northern end. The Kusel houses (cat. 44) were clearly modeled on the former, while the unidentified attached house (cat. 40) resembles the latter. Many other buildings were based on these designs, which provided a limited range of architectural elements and a set example of proportions. Only very slight modifications, necessary to emphasize entrances or major rooms, were allowed.

Weinbrenner's control over almost all residential construction was exerted through the *Baugnade*, or building grant—a scheme that Karl Friedrich, persuaded by Weinbrenner, established in 1804. Every builder who erected a house according to Weinbrenner's prescriptions would receive a fixed sum from the state's coffers, the amount varying according to the position of the building within the city, the width of the facade, the number of stories, and so forth. This financial incentive was intended to accelerate completion of the city, while establishing and maintaining a uniformity of appearance. Building grants were not new; they had been instituted in Karlsruhe in 1752,[10] and in intent they were similar to the peppercorn rents set by London landlords to encourage building on their property. In Berlin and Potsdam grants were also given to control street fronts, while in Stuttgart free wood and sometimes even building lots were given away as incentives. The differences between these and the Karlsruhe *Baugnade* of 1804 lay in the degree of control. Most similar schemes were intended to define street lines and the projection and height of buildings in order to avoid sanitation problems and fire risks. The 1804 scheme for Karlsruhe included provisions for these matters but went much further in actively encouraging private builders to accept Weinbrenner's model designs.

Voluntary building grants were enforced in Karlsruhe by the *Baupolizei*, or building inspectorate, whose aims were supported and proselytized by Weinbrenner. The *Baupolizei* watched over the maintenance of buildings and the salubrity of living conditions, and they also compelled, if necessary, the use of proper design models for "people of all classes."[11]

Despite partial success of the 1804 design, it soon became apparent that models of greater flexibility had to be found if the city were to respond to its varied needs. In 1814 and 1815 Weinbrenner accordingly produced a veritable blueprint for every variety of residential living.[12] These new model facades were more concerned with establishing the relationship between groups of town houses of different heights than with defining the details of openings and facade treatment, as had been the case in the

1804 designs. Although that earlier essay in wholesale standardization had had its antecedent in his own "General Bauplan," an extensive replanning project of 1797, Weinbrenner now moved away from that proposal's barrack-like monotony.[13] The new design divided residences into three types: one- and two-story houses for manual and factory workers in the outlying districts; two- and three-story houses for the middle class in the central areas; and two-, three-, four-, and even five-story houses for "wealthy individuals in the pre-eminent districts and main streets."[14] There is, however, no evidence that any five-story houses were built, and records show that two-story houses far outnumbered all others.[15] The composition of grouped houses was much more relaxed than in the earlier designs, although it was still responsive to the formality of major intersections and public squares. Individual houses were dignified by balconies, pediments, and recessed arches, and even in houses of the first type, pilasters were applied to the upper stories. Continuity was secured by consistent roof lines and stringcourses, but most dramatically by a striding ground-level arcade in the houses of the third type. This arcade was reminiscent of the even more spectacular three-story arcade with which Weinbrenner intended to mask the existing houses on the Lange Strasse in 1806,[16] although the device was now subdued to an urban mannerliness redolent of Percier and Fontaine's rue de Rivoli (1802–55).

The difficulty of reversing even a hundred years of development and creating consistency of style and grouping was such that Weinbrenner, despite his great apparatus of control, accomplished little outside the major intersections and squares. An 1826 panorama shows that Karlsruhe was still a town of abruptly uneven house heights and irregular development.[17] This is evident on a major street such as the Lange Strasse, and in Weinbrenner's most complete transformation, the Marktplatz, where the northeastern corner was still filled by older two-story houses. One should not assume that Weinbrenner always had power over the appearance of individual streets and groups of houses. In one important case, opposition from a group of building contractors secured for them from the grand duke a relaxation of Weinbrenner's limitations on house heights; hence, for example, three-story houses were allowed on the Stephanienstrasse.[18]

Successful or not, Weinbrenner's argument was not based on safety or salubrity. His analysis was directed instead by his sense of esthetic propriety. Many of the plates in his *Architektonisches Lehrbuch* attest to this in their concern for vistas, seen both from eye level and from above, in which sight lines are monumentalized in the crests of pediments and roofs and in the arrises and planes of buildings.[19]

The measure of architectural cohesiveness that Weinbrenner did achieve in Karlsruhe was knowingly broken at critical points by higher or lower buildings and by setbacks and projections. A calm, even pseudorural expansiveness was suggested by the punctuation of the Schloss Strasse by the villa-like Beck house (fig. 5, cat. 37), and by the siting of Weinbrenner's own country house-like residence (cats. 35, 36) beside an outer gate of the city. In quieter residential streets, such as the Zähringerstrasse, the monotony of rowhouses was occasionally broken by a gable turned toward the street,[20] or by repressing one bay to emphasize the verticalness of a facade.[21] Typically, corner sites were guarded by a tower motif, sometimes disguised by pilasters and a pediment,[22] or reduced to a turret (cat. 39), or, more rarely, made explicitly four-square and capped with a hipped roof.[23] In another instance a pair of pedimented houses were linked by a triumphal arch guarding the entry into their shared courtyard.[24]

Weinbrenner's treatment of the town house as an integral yet varied part of its urban context bears comparison to the work of two of his German contemporaries, Karl von Fischer in Munich and Georg Laves in Hanover. Munich, an older city than Karlsruhe, had gained new importance with the establishment of the kingdom of Bavaria in 1806. The Vienna-trained Fischer (1782–1820), who held a position there like Weinbrenner's, was employed to modernize the city in his refined Palladian style. In the planning of the Briennerstrasse (1806–14), and particularly the circular Karolinenplatz (1808), Fischer disposed his buildings in free-standing blocks set in generous park-like grounds, an arrangement reminiscent of Ledoux's plan for the ideal town of Chaux, but quite unlike Weinbrenner, who preferred more wholeheartedly urban solutions.[25] Georg Laves (1788–1864) developed a free-standing villa type in Hanover, surrounding it by informal gardens, with an effect reminiscent of the Beck house.[26] However, Laves emphasized the blocklike integrity and verticalness of his designs more than Weinbrenner, and in this sense his work was closer to English Palladianism. By contrast with the work of both Fischer and Laves, the continuous wall surfaces of Weinbrenner's adjacent town houses seem claustrophobic; the buildings are drawn up firmly to the street line and allow only controlled views of the distant Grand Ducal Palace.

The astute resolution of difficult planning problems has always been seen as one of Weinbrenner's salient qualities. For the medium-sized rowhouse on a straightforward rectangular site, he employed a stock solution in which the staircase was situated at the center rear, the passage to the courtyard was cut against the side wall, and the major rooms lined the front of the principal upper floor (cat. 40). An axis was drawn through connecting doors across these formal reception rooms, terminating at each end in a shallow, doorlike cavity in the party wall. Privies usually were located in the spare spaces beside the staircase, which would often project as a bay into the courtyard (checklist 54.2). On the major streets the ground floor of these houses would be given over to shop space. Most were designed for at least two families.

Karlsruhe's radial plan also abounded in much more difficult corner sites and a variety of awkward, irregular lots; here, Weinbrenner's powers were tested

Fig. 5. Reutlinger House on the Rondellplatz, with Jöslin and Beck Houses adjoining at left, c. 1910. (*Stadtarchiv, XIIb 261*)

more severely. His most common solution for ninety-degree corner sites placed the staircase at a diagonal to the corner, arrayed the rooms along the street fronts, and placed the entrances well along the sides (as in the first Kusel house, cat. 44, and in the inn, checklist 64.1). On acute-angled sites, a turret often filled the corner and linked the two enfilades (cat. 39).[27] The rowhouse solution was adapted to a crooked site by moving the staircase to one side and combining a group of unusual room shapes around a courtyard (cat. 43). With the exception of the *Kabinett*, usually a circular room used to exhibit the most precious of personal possessions, the geometrical shapes had little to do with the definition of

particular functions, or at least not in the terms of the elaborate social parade fostered earlier by planning like that of Robert Adam in England. Rather, Weinbrenner's town-house planning was based on the pragmatic adaptation of Palladian norms to the exigencies of awkward sites. This frequently meant that not every room had its own access to the entrance hall, and dining rooms sometimes had to be reached through kitchens or even bedrooms.

On larger corner sites Weinbrenner, influenced by French hotels, occasionally placed the main entrance at the angle itself, driving a passage wide enough for a carriage straight through the house to the courtyard. This plan proved adaptable for different building types and was used for both the Karlsruhe Museum and the Hertzer house in Baden-Baden (cats. 45, 46).[28] In all these corner plans an atrium-like space furnished light to the access passages and staircases at the rear of the building. In the Hertzer house the atrium was the largest room in the design, and in others it was canopied by a dome.[29]

The plans of these houses, like their elevations, were typified by the play of variations on a limited number of themes. Their effect relied on the adjustment of proportions, the ability of parts to retain their independence in a coherent whole, and the restraint and economy of emphasis. In its circumscribed variety, controlled through Weinbrenner's grip on building legislation and the widespread application of his model facades, his domestic architecture mirrored its bourgeois clientele.

NOTES

1. For constitutional reforms in Baden, see Gall (1968); Lee (1980); Liebel (1965); Weller (1979).
2. Lee (1980, 17–28).
3. J. Mall, ed., *Adressbuch der Haupt- und Residenzstadt Carlsruhe* (Karlsruhe: C. T. Groos, 1832).
4. For charts tabulating the quantities and distribution of houses, see Ehrenberg (1908, 99).
5. Information from town maps of 1780, 1802, 1810, 1817, 1823, and 1834 is in the Landesdenkmalamt, Karlsruhe.
6. Illustrated in Koebel ([1920], 65).
7. Photograph of 77 Zähringerstrasse is in the Landesdenkmalamt, Karlsruhe, microfilm no. K4593, negative no. 0729.
8. Ehrenberg (1908, 99).
9. Valdenaire (1919 [2d ed., 1926, 100]).
10. Ehrenberg (1908, 79).
11. Weinbrenner, "Baupolizei im Allgemein," in Weinbrenner (1926, 17–18).

12. Staatliche Kunsthalle (1977, 109); Valdenaire (1919 [2d ed., 1926, 81ff.]).
13. Exactly this kind of effect was later attacked by Weinbrenner; see Huber (1954, 81).
14. Valdenaire (1919 [2d ed., 1926, 83]).
15. Three-story houses were erected increasingly toward the end of this period; see Ehrenberg (1908, 99).
16. Valdenaire (1919 [2d ed., 1926, 86]).
17. Original in the Landesdenkmalamt, Karlsruhe.
18. Huber (1954, 39ff).
19. See, for example, Weinbrenner (1810–25, vol. 2, fasc. 6, 37, 42).
20. Examples are the Sommerschuh house and the first project for the Holb house (cat. 41).
21. An example is the house at 77 Zähringerstrasse.
22. An example is the house on the corner of the Lange Strasse and the Waldhornstrasse; see Valdenaire (1919 [2d ed., 1926, 130–31]).
23. An example is the house on the Ludwigsplatz; see Koebel ([1920], 67).
24. Examples are the Bodmer house and the General von Lingg house, built 1811–12 by C. T. Fischer after a design by Weinbrenner; see the photograph in the Landesdenkmalamt, Karlsruhe, microfilm no. K4580, negative no. 0723, and the drawing in Koebel ([1920], 69).
25. For Karl von Fischer, see Winfried Nerdinger, ed., *Klassizismus in Bayern, Schwaben, und Franken: Architektur-Zeichnungen, 1775–1825* (Munich: Stadtmuseum, 1980); and Ilse Springorum-Kleiner, *Karl von Fischer, 1782–1820* (Munich: Uni-Druck, 1982).
26. An example is the house on the Friedrichstrasse (1821–22), in Georg Hoeltje and Helmut Weber, *Georg Ludwig Laves* (Hanover: Steinbock, 1964), 77.
27. See also the design for a private house in *Sammlung* (1847–58, 14).
28. The evolution of the museum plan can be studied in Geier (n.d.).
29. The house, for example, at 47 Karlstrasse is illustrated in Geier (n.d.) and *Sammlung* (1847–58, 18).

The New Imagery of Public Architecture

Robert Wojtowicz and David B. Brownlee

THE FAMOUS pin factory that Adam Smith described in the *Wealth of Nations* (1776), where each worker concentrated on a small part of the manufacturing process, exemplified the division of labor and the specialization of modern industrial society. In architecture a contemporary corollary could be found in the invention of myriad new building types that served the specialized needs of the rising middle class. While Friedrich Weinbrenner built several churches and remodeled the Grand Ducal Palace, most of his public commissions were of this new kind. He designed theaters, baths, casinos, schools, inns, tombs, and greenhouses for the bourgeoisie of Karlsruhe; fountains and a town hall for their city government; and the mint, barracks, legislative hall, and chancellery for the bureaucratic apparatus of their state. One of the greatest challenges of his professional life was to find the means of expressing this new variety of architectural form.

Weinbrenner's experiments identified alternative solutions that would be tested and retested for one hundred years. Initially, it seemed to him that the late eighteenth-century flowering of modern architectural history—the rediscovery of Greek and Gothic architecture and the immensely more scientific investigation of Roman antiquity—could provide a vocabulary sufficiently varied to proclaim the characters of these new types. This belief in the complementary relationship between the expression of architectural types and the growth of historical scholarship became one of the controversial credos of nineteenth-century design. But in the course of his career, Weinbrenner himself abandoned such his-

toricist eclecticism in favor of an adaptable, less specifically meaningful species of classicism. This nascent antihistoricism was the other strand from which decades of subsequent debate would be woven.

Weinbrenner, drawing on literature and what he had seen during his student travels, strove to fashion a modern architectural idiom. He had studied Palladio and seen Greek and Roman antiquity; he knew the Gothic of his homeland and a variety of exotic Oriental architectural styles that he had never seen. These forms gave him the semantic palette with which he first experimented.

For Weinbrenner the meaning conveyed by antiquity's classical forms was forever colored by his extended sojourn in Italy (1792–97). His experience there had been influenced by the scale and grandeur in the etchings of Piranesi, but where the Italian artist had seen ruins, the young German architect saw potential models for modern building types. During his stay in Italy he became preoccupied with the reintroduction of ancient classicism to Baden, which had been part of the Roman Empire. One of Weinbrenner's first projects was a hypothetical reconstruction of the Roman bath at Badenweiler, less than 150 kilometers southwest of Karlsruhe; he sketched many projects for classical public buildings during his student years, intending to return imperial dignity to his native city.

The classicism Weinbrenner espoused was highly inventive and often diverged from Vitruvian principles. Having arrived in Rome a generation after the Piranesi-Winckelmann debates over the comparative merits of Greek and Roman architecture, he was not concerned about purity of form or traditional rules governing proportion. Although he repeatedly used the baseless Doric columns he had seen at Paestum in various early projects, he often mixed them with non-Greek forms. They appeared, for example, in a design for a riding school in Karlsruhe, which improbably assumed the plan of a Roman basilica (cats. 57, 58). In the courtyard of his proposed arsenal, Doric columns and entablatures were similarly juxtaposed with arches and piers, within a building type whose plan and massing were decidedly Roman (cats. 47, 48).

Weinbrenner's interest in the antique was not confined to architecture. The loose and rather clumsy sketch on the verso of one of the riding-school drawings—that of the drinking contest between Herakles and Dionysus—reveals not only an interest in the mythology of the ancients but also an appreciation of the classical nude (cat. 58). The sketch also alludes to the kind of amusement enjoyed by the architectural student and his artistic comrades in the eternal city, as he fondly recalled in his autobiography.[1] This, too, was the meaning of antiquity.

Upon returning to Germany in 1797 Weinbrenner must have quickly realized that his grandiose, classical student projects alone could not provide models for the variety of commissions that came to him. For his first public buildings he broadened his stylistic repertoire to include the broad range of medieval and modern architecture with which he was familiar, and it was through this often flamboyant inventiveness that he quickly rose to prominence within the staid architectural community still dominated by Jeremias Müller, his predecessor as building director. The primary example of this eclecticism was Weinbrenner's formidable design of 1798 for the Karlsruhe synagogue (cat. 50). Faced with an irregular site on one of the oblique corners of the radial city, and given a complex agenda for a multipurpose structure, he drew upon the whole history of architecture. Because a synagogue seemed to be a building type without strong ties to any architectural past, he felt free to design the structure in a com-

bination of styles, including Egyptian (reflecting the eastern character of Judaism), Greek, Roman, early Christian, and Gothic. In his proposal for a Turkish bath, although he was probably commissioned to design an ordinary steam bath, he transformed the utilitarian structure by clothing it with the Ottoman imagery appropriate to its function (cat. 59). The same motivation led him to design a Gothic tower in 1802 on Margravine Amalie's estate for use as a chapel (cat. 9), and to employ the model of a medieval fortress for his Karlsruhe powder magazine in 1806. In these designs one can see the germ of the nineteenth-century belief that certain styles were appropriate to certain building types.

Weinbrenner's buildings after 1807 do not exhibit the same eclectic freedom. As he won an increasing number of commissions it became obvious that no ransacking of the past, no matter how thorough, could provide enough models for the proliferation of building types. Thus while the towers of his great public buildings—the Rathaus (1805–25), the Evangelische Stadtkirche (1807–16), and the Katholische Stadtkirche (1808–14)—give Karlsruhe an almost medieval profile, their details are classical. Only subtle allusions remained as a sign of his initial semantic experiments, borne on the back of a broad and no longer very meaningful classicism. Significantly, none of Weinbrenner's eclectic designs found its way into the *Lehrbuch*.

The mainstay of Weinbrenner's architecture became the filtered classicism of Andrea Palladio (cat. 80). This was not wholly reactionary, for Palladio had been much admired by late eighteenth-century French and English architects, and the revival of his characteristic style laid the foundation of the neoclassical movement. Moreover, the Vicentine master was a particularly appropriate model for Weinbrenner, since he was one of the first Renaissance architects to experiment freely with antique forms, and his work pointed toward an acceptable way of adapting the grandeur of ancient classicism for Karlsruhe. Weinbrenner had produced several gargantuan villa projects based on Palladian models while in Rome,

Fig. 6. Victory monument, Leipzig. (*Weinbrenner [1814]*)

and the country houses that he built for the aristocracy of Karlsruhe followed this example (see cats.
1–3). His designs for the new building types of the
bourgeoisie also reflected the influence of Palladio,
as seen in the porticoed Karlsruhe theater (1807–8),
and more generally in the Rathaus and his large city
churches, in which neoclassical forms were concate-
nated in a typically Palladian way. Individual Palladian features, like thermal windows placed within
pediments and tympana supported by pairs of columns, could be found in even simple projects, such
as the Promenadenhaus (1814–15) and the Stepha-
nienbad at nearby Beiertheim (1814–17).

Compromised, Palladianized, and modernized,
the antique heritage of Weinbrenner's later classicism
was much diluted. Only in his designs for public
monuments and war memorials did he continue to
demonstrate his enduring interest in the meaningful-

ness of ancient forms, or in the semantic weight of
architecture in general. This was uniquely possible
in projects that lacked practical programs—that consisted of meaning alone.

Although Baden was a French ally–even vassal–
during the first half of Weinbrenner's career, and
while he designed a monument to Napoleon's Grand
Armée in 1806, he was evidently proudest of two
proposals for Greco-Roman monuments that celebrated the defeat of France and the emergence of a
German national identity. The first of these memori-
alized the Battle of Leipzig in 1813, the French
defeat that compelled Baden to join the anti-
Napoleonic alliance. Weinbrenner accommodated
himself to the new state of affairs quickly and celebrated what he saw as a German victory with a
proposal for a colossal monument (fig. 6, cat. 55). It
borrowed heavily from the reconstruction of the

Mausoleum at Halicarnassus that he had drawn while in Rome. "This monument should raise the general patriotic sense which alone can maintain one nation in its independence," he wrote fervently; "in order to propagate this common spirit for eternity, nothing can be too costly for the German people."[2] Despite his enthusiasm the Leipzig memorial went unbuilt, as did his intentionally simpler and cheaper design for a monument to mark the final Napoleonic defeat at Waterloo (cat. 56).

The legacy of Weinbrenner's public architecture was complex. Some of the first generation to pass through his school—including Friedrich Arnold and Georg Moller—simply emulated the rather bland classicism of his major buildings. But others, who surprisingly were among those whose interest turned to German Romanesque and Gothic architecture, recognized the essentially styleless rationalism of his mature work. Their intellectual leader was Heinrich Hübsch, and his *Rundbogenstil*'s synthesis of Renaissance and Romanesque forms was founded on the premise that the various architectural styles could not convey discrete meanings. That was something Friedrich Weinbrenner had already discovered.

NOTES

1. Weinbrenner (1958, 99–100).
2. Weinbrenner (1814, 10).

In the Shadow of
Imperial France:
The Redecoration of
the Grand Ducal Palace

David B. Brownlee
with assistance from
Leslie Blacksberg

FRIEDRICH Weinbrenner redecorated the west wing of the Karlsruhe Palace early in the reign of Grand Duke Karl and Grand Duchess Stephanie, who ruled Baden between 1811 and 1818. Most of the physical evidence of this vast undertaking was altered by another building campaign between 1854 and 1856, and the few surviving fragments, together with the interior ornamentation of nearly all of Weinbrenner's other buildings, were destroyed in the Allied bombing of 1944. The only substantial record of the commission—and the fullest documentation of any of Weinbrenner's decorative work—is in Philadelphia, where there are eleven drawings that can be securely associated with his plans for the palace (cats. 60–67, checklist 218.1–218.11) and another fifty-nine related sheets (cat. 68 and checklist 210.1–210.29, 226.1–226.20, 242.1–242.10.). This unique body of material consists largely of pencil drawings, apparently from Weinbrenner's own hand, and it affords an unmatched glimpse of his proclivities as a decorative artist. The drawings also portray the setting created for the court of Baden in one of its most troubled hours, when, having linked its fate with Napoleon's, the grand duchy was compelled to taste some of the bitterness of his defeat.

Weinbrenner brought to this commission great experience in the design problems of the decorative arts. He returned permanently to Karlsruhe in 1800, by which time he had devoted twelve years of study to the art of architecture, having traveled across Austria, Germany, and Switzerland to Italy. It was in Rome, the international capital of neoclassicism, that he learned the morphemes of the modern decorative vocabulary. By the time Weinbrenner arrived there on September 1, 1792, the new syntax had been thoroughly explored. The wonders of Roman wall painting, as seen in the plenitude of examples from the Domus Aurea, had been familiar since the Renaissance, and there were also myriad paintings uncovered by the excavations at Herculaneum and Pompeii. The generation of Robert Adam had already carried an understanding of these forms northward in the 1750s and 1760s.

For Weinbrenner's contemporaries it was not such Roman grotesque work but the rediscovery of Greek art that was new, and his excursions to Paestum and the praise that fills his *Lehrbuch* testify to his interest. But while stubby Greek Doric columns gave vigor to many of his earliest architectural designs (cats. 38, 50, 57, 58), there was no comparable Greek influence to be traced in his decoration. That Greece could inspire decor was left to be discovered by the more ardent revivalists who followed him. Weinbrenner's work as a decorator, while strong, thus appears relatively conservative (cat. 13). His motifs were Roman, his colors were Pompeiian, and his interiors as a whole seem to have been filtered through the kind of shared Italian experience that also informed the work of his great French contemporaries, Charles Percier and Pierre Fontaine, the creators of Napoleon's imperial art—the Empire Style. Theirs were the last decades of eighteenth-century neoclassicism, carried somewhat uncertainly into the more critical period after 1800.

Weinbrenner's student years in Italy, when his art was formed, are the best documented part of his life. Most of his autobiographical fragment deals with his Italian adventures, and a large number of his travel drawings have been preserved.[1] Yet there is little among these records concerning the decorative arts. His memoirs are vague, recounting, for example:

> While I was again living for about three months in Naples and its environs [on my second visit, in 1796], I made for myself some now lost sketches of those interesting antiquities of which one cannot obtain engravings—especially [sketches] of the decorations and beautiful mosaics in Portici and Pompeii, where it is difficult to get permission to copy.[2]

Only a study of his subsequent architectural work can demonstrate that he had paid special heed to the Ara Pacis (cat. 68) and the Domus Aurea in Rome (cat. 70) or that he had studied the Pompeiian painting fragments now in Naples (cat. 66). Such interests were apparently so ordinary that they merited no comment, and in that context the verve of some of his designs comes as a surprise (cat. 71). Even the sheer variety of ornamental language invented for the Grand Ducal Palace still has the power to astonish.

The beginnings of the palace in Karlsruhe had been modest but auspicious.[3] On July 17, 1715, Margrave Karl Wilhelm of Baden-Durlach laid the foundation stone for a country residence called "Carols Ruh" (Karl's Rest). It stood at the center of thirty-two radiating *allées* that sliced northward into the hunting preserve of the Hardtwald and southward (as streets) into the new capital he founded at the same time. Karl Wilhelm's architect was Jacob Friedrich von Batzendorf, who created for his patron a vast two-story building surmounted by a mansard roof. At the very center of the city's radiating plan rose the octagonal tower of the palace, connected by a gallery to the *corps de logis* lying to its south. This main block was attached to east and west wings that opened outward at oblique angles to embrace the small city. The building was largely of traditional half-timbered construction, although this was disguised by stucco and sheathing. South of the palace, between its two arms, lay a formal, French-style garden, the source of much pride on the part of Karl Wilhelm, an amateur botanist who had studied in Holland. The margrave's new residence, created at one with its urban and botanical surroundings, was the perfect image of late baroque artistic and political absolutism.

The long reign of Karl Wilhelm's successor Karl Friedrich began in 1746, after an eight-year regency, and the rebuilding of the wooden palace occupied much of his attention during its first years. Starting in 1749 a series of designs was prepared by Leopoldo Retti, Mauricio Pedetti, Philippe de la Guépière, and Balthasar Neumann; these were evaluated and compared, but the commission was finally awarded to Albert Friedrich von Kesslau, who had studied with La Guépière in Paris. Construction began in 1752, and while the general plan of the old building was retained, thus preserving its almost primitive ungainliness, a pavilion was inserted where each side wing joined the main block. This softened their conjunction. The entire palace, except the tower, was rebuilt. The exterior was complete by 1770, and the interior in 1775. In 1785 Jeremias Müller, the *Baudirektor* under whom Weinbrenner would begin his career, reconstructed the tower and topped it with a more firmly contoured dome (figs. 7, 8).

Karl Friedrich and his first wife, Margravine Karoline Luise, were ardent Francophiles. They ordered furnishings for the rebuilt palace from Paris, and they commissioned replicas of other French designs to be made in Baden. The disposition of rooms within the palace, however, followed the elaborate etiquette established at the Viennese court.[4] Only courtiers of the highest rank could penetrate beyond the representational rooms and the great Marmorsaal, located above the main entrance in the central block. The private apartments of the mar-

Fig. 7. Grand Ducal Palace, garden facade, c. 1935. (*Stadtarchiv, XIVa 1088*)

grave and margravine were located on two floors in the west wing, with the finest rooms concentrated in the northwest angle pavilion. Its windows commanded views into the grounds that Karl Friedrich had had remade in the English landscape style. The margrave also had summer apartments in the northeast pavilion.

The palace was the scene for the multitudinous festivities required by courtly life: balls, name-day celebrations, and hunting parties. But the court in Karlsruhe had a serious side as well, with hospitality extended to Voltaire, Goethe, and a host of other luminaries with whom Karl Friedrich maintained regular correspondence.

As the nineteenth century dawned and Karl Fried-

rich passed into his seventies, the brilliance of the court at Karlsruhe was somewhat dimmed. Baden had fought against France's republican armies, but with the rise of Napoleon neutrality became the only prudent course for the tiny state. In 1806, after a period of increasing French dependence, she was drafted into an alliance with the emperor as a member of the Rhine Confederation. Alliance made Baden a grand duchy and brought enormous territorial accessions, but her soldiers were drafted into the Napoleonic armies, her finances were governed from Paris, and the details of official life were overseen ever more strictly from afar.

The most galling symbol of this intervention was Napoleon's insistence that Karl Friedrich's grandson

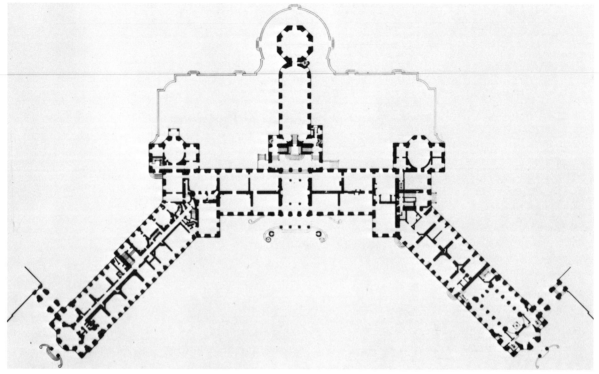

Fig. 8. Grand Ducal Palace, ground floor plan. (*Badisches Landesmuseum*)

and heir apparent, Karl, break off his engagement with Princess Augusta of Bavaria. He matched the young man instead with Stephanie de Beauharnais, the second cousin of Empress Josephine's first husband, whom Napoleon had adopted as a daughter. In January 1806, on the eve of the formation of the Rhine Confederation, the emperor visited Karlsruhe to confirm his wishes, and the two were married on April 8 in the Tuileries. Margravine Amalie, Karl's mother, objected strenuously but in vain.

Karl and Stephanie had a dreary marriage.[5] The crown prince was a dull man who could not be lured away from the debauchery of his youth by an unwanted wife, and she found life in Baden unspeakably boring after her experience in the imperial household. She knew Percier and Fontaine's *dernière cri* at Malmaison and the Tuileries and found nothing comparable in Karlsruhe. Later in life she recorded the thoughts of her first morning in the little capital:

> Upon waking, I was most astonished to find such an unhandsome town. What had seemed in the evening, by lamplight, to be beautiful palaces, were only little wooden houses. They have been rebuilt since then in stone, but they are still humble dwellings, lacking in architecture.[6]

The couple chose to live apart. When not with his troops in the east Karl lived in the Grand Ducal Palace or with his mother at Bruchsal (cat. 16), and Stephanie maintained a separate establishment in the great baroque residence at Mannheim. She was able to return to Paris several times, and she traveled to see Napoleon and Josephine whenever they passed through Germany. So cool was her treatment in Baden that Napoleon threatened to recall her to Paris, and as a result some of Karl's less reputable companions were sent away.

The health of the grand duke deteriorated, and the impending succession seems to have brought Karl and Stephanie together at last in 1810. They gradually joined their two households, and although they continued to dine separately (he at 12:30 and she at 5:00), their first child was born in 1811, just four days before Karl Friedrich died on July 10 at the age of eighty-three.

The new grand duchess moved into the Karlsruhe Palace in August 1811. Although a few neoclassical interiors had been inserted late in the eighteenth century, and although Weinbrenner had refitted the chapel in 1801 and the throne room in 1806, most of the rooms in the more habitable west wing of the palace were still decorated on Von Kesslau's late rococo style, which was now hopelessly out of date. Weinbrenner consequently was retained to remake many of the rooms on the western ground floor, including the northwest pavilion where Stephanie's principal apartments were located (cat. 60). The work began in the winter of 1811–12, but it went ahead under the most unpromising conditions.[7] Baden's troops were decimated in the Napoleonic Russian campaign of 1812 and 1813–only 140 from a contingent of 7,166 were still alive on December 30—and most of her remaining forces were killed or imprisoned at the Battle of Leipzig in October 1813. On November 20 Karl was compelled to join the anti-French alliance of Austria, Russia, and Prussia, leading poor Stephanie to exclaim, "I am entering a wholly new world."[8]

Nevertheless, the products of Weinbrenner's labors were impressive. For Stephanie's suite he created his own variations on Empire-Style themes, selecting those motifs from his own repertoire that were closest to what she would have seen in Paris. He evidently strove to recreate some of the effects represented in Percier and Fontaine's *Recueil de décorations intérieures* (1801), although his interpretations were inevitably somewhat drier and he declined to fill the decorative field as densely as they did. The resulting decoration in the Grand Ducal Palace was far more linear in detail than his work elsewhere, although the paucity of comparanda prohibits definitive conclusions. This is particularly apparent in the ceilings, which comprise an anthology of Robert Adam-like grotesques, some rendered in a dancing pencil line while others are firmed by a sharp trace of ink (cat. 68).

It is likely that Weinbrenner's interiors were in place before the Battle of Leipzig (October 1813), for thereafter the battered finances of the court, long subsidized by Napoleon, could not have sustained such extravagances. The effect of his work was recorded sketchily in an inventory of 1814, which reported the color schemes, furnishings, and uses of some rooms, including the Grau Salon, which was used as a library (fig. 9).[9] Karl's mother and his sisters (the queens of Sweden and Bavaria and the czarina of Russia) inspected the new appointments on May 28, 1814, and that summer Eugène and Hortense Beauharnais also visited Baden.[10] Stephanie's French relatives were probably surprised to find how well the grand duchess now lived. In this setting Stephanie even enjoyed something like the ordinary joys of marriage; next to her oval drawing room, with its views of the garden, Weinbrenner created a billiard room for the grand duke.

Karl attended the Vienna conference that decided the structure of post-Napoleonic Europe in the winter of 1814–15. His neglect of affairs of state caused some comment among the diplomats, and he fell seriously ill. Although his condition rebounded occasionally during the next few years, he never fully regained his health. He became obsessed with the

Fig. 9. Grand Ducal Palace, Grau Salon, after installation of the Badisches Landesmuseum in 1919 and before the Second World War. (*Stadtarchiv, XIVa 1018*)

fear of being poisoned, a concern made more understandable by the precarious line of succession, which was restricted to male heirs. His first son had died before receiving a name in 1812, and Alexander, his second, had died in 1817 just after his first birthday. In that year Stephanie's last pregnancy produced a third daughter. With these morose prospects Karl sank slowly toward death. On December 31, 1817,

he appeared in public for the last time, and he finally died on December 8, 1818. Although the new constitution was promulgated during his last months of life, Karl took little interest in it, and its implementation was left to his successor and uncle, the unmarried Grand Duke Ludwig. Upon Ludwig's death in 1830, the line of succession shifted to the Hochbergs, the children of Karl Friedrich's second wife, Luise Geyer von Geyersberg. Baden's Napo-leonic alliances, marital and military, had led to this melancholy end.

NOTES

1. Staatliche Kunsthalle (1978, nos. 4364–4401); Schneider (1961).
2. Weinbrenner (1958, 125).
3. For the palace's general history, see Gutman (1911), Kircher (1959), Stratmann (1976 [2d ed., 1982]), Stratmann (1980), Valdenaire (1931).
4. Markgräflich Badische Museen (1981, 88–100); Badisches Landesmuseum, Karlsruhe, *Caroline Luise, Markgräfin von Baden, 1723–1783* (Stuttgart: Konrad Theiss, 1983), 123–56.
5. For this period, see Françoise de Bernardy, *Stéphanie de Beauharnais (1789–1860), Fille adoptive de Napoléon, Grand-duchesse de Bade*, 3d ed. (Paris: Perrin, 1977); Rudolf Haas, *Stephanie Napoleon, Grossherzogin von Baden: Ein Leben zwischen Frankreich und Deutschland, 1789–1860* (Mannheim: Südwestdeutsche Verlagsan-stalt, 1976); Robert Roquette, "Stéphanie-Napoléon," *Etudes* 304 (January–March 1960): 308–26; *Etudes* 305 (April–June 1960): 41–47; and Friedrich Walter, *Stéphanie-Napoléon: Lebensweg und Weggenossen, 1789–1860* (Baden-Baden: Drei-Kreise Verlag, [1949]).
6. Countess H. de Reinach Foussemagne, ed., "Sou-venirs de Stéphanie de Beauharnais, Grande-duchesse de Bade," *Revue des deux mondes* 8s, 8 (March–April 1932): 101.
7. Bauakten, Generallandesarchiv, Karlsruhe, 2976.
8. Bernardy, op. cit., 138.
9. Generallandesarchiv, Karlsruhe, 56/4098.
10. Hoftagebücher, Generallandesarchiv, Karlsruhe, 47/2057.

The Birth of a German Academic Tradition

Michael J. Lewis

THE 1790S were the formative decade of Friedrich Weinbrenner's career as well as a decisive decade for German architecture. One cannot speak of a German architecture before that time in the same sense that one speaks of a characteristic French or English form of that art. In part, this was the consequence of Germany's political division into a multitude of sovereign states.[1] While notable architects worked in Berlin, Munich, Stuttgart, Kassel and other cities, none of these possessed the national cultural primacy of London or Paris. Until the founding of the Berlin Bauakademie in 1799, there was also no truly national architectural school, and a comprehensive architectural education could only be had abroad or in the office of one of the French emigré architects occasionally summoned to German cities. What distinction German architecture had at this time was the result of regional vernacular patrimony, not the product of an indigenous intellectual or professional tradition.

Weinbrenner's architectural education coincided with the birth of such an indigenous architectural tradition in Germany. Like other architects of his generation, he grappled with issues such as the nature of classical and medieval architecture, the concept of architectural character, and the role of materials and construction in the art of architecture. His resolution of these questions—as expressed in the *Architektonisches Lehrbuch* (cats. 73–79) and other theoretical writings—influenced much of the course of nineteenth-century German architecture.

Although his early education had been that of a practically trained builder, Weinbrenner overcame his late start with six years of intense architectural study and archaeological research in the company of some of the most prominent German-speaking men of letters. His training as a carpenter, acting as bridle and spur, disciplined his later theoretical studies. It motivated his experiments with structural systems and restrained him when academic theory threatened to contradict his understanding of materials and their assembly. In this respect he resembled the elder David Gilly (1748–1808), and not Gilly's son Friedrich (1772–1800), who had an almost Jacobin fascination for the heroic rather than the pragmatic.

The background for the formulation of Weinbrenner's theory was the rediscovery of ancient Greek architecture and the recognition that it surpassed Roman and Renaissance classicism in its vigor and tectonic logic. This rediscovery was still electrifying the architectural circles of Berlin and Rome in the 1790s, the two cities where the kernel of Weinbrenner's theory was developed. It was Berlin that led Germany in promoting the archaeological study of Greek remains, as well as in reviving the heavy, primitive forms of early Greek Doric architecture. This taste was paralleled by contemporary French architecture, which had influenced building in Berlin since Jean-Laurent Legeay had worked there at mid-century.[2] But by the time of Weinbrenner's arrival in 1792, Berlin's young architects had already assimilated the lessons of their French tutors; Greek taste no longer needed to be imported from Paris but was being tapped at its wellspring, in the ancient Greek sites of southern Italy and Sicily. There, since the late 1780s, Berlin architects such as Heinrich Gentz and Hans Christian Genelli had carried on intensive archaeological investigation.

It was Genelli (1763–1823) who introduced Weinbrenner to Greek taste—the "Paestum style" Weinbrenner later called it—and to the higher issues of architectural theory. Before meeting him Weinbrenner was still beholden to mid-eighteenth-century French taste, both in manners and architecture, and still wore the wig he had bought on his arrival in Berlin to make himself look "dashing."[3] Genelli opened Weinbrenner's eyes to Berlin's neo-classical architecture; the scholarly Berliner and Weinbrenner, the artisan, complemented one another, as Weinbrenner later recalled:

> I had the fortune to become acquainted with, and to befriend, the local architect Genelli who had just returned from Rome. Through the friendship of this cultured man I learned more for myself than I perhaps might have otherwise in a course of public instruction. Genelli, whose company I enjoyed daily during my stay, and I had gone in diametrically opposed directions in our training as architects. He began the study of architecture according to its theory and history at roughly the same time that I began from the bottom, namely with its practical application.[4]

Genelli weaned Weinbrenner away from the French architecture whose forms he had copied in his earliest designs, and Weinbrenner's most important project in Berlin—a modern church based on a Doric reinterpretation of the Pantheon—shows how rapidly the seed planted by Genelli sprouted.[5] Weinbrenner came to appreciate the purified, stripped forms of Doric architecture because of the man who was their principal apostle in Berlin. With his proposal of 1788 for a monument to Frederick the Great, Genelli had introduced the baseless Doric column to German architecture. Although this remained unbuilt, Genelli's example set the key for Karl Gotthard Langhans's updating of the Propylea in his Brandenburg Gate. Completed at about the time of Weinbrenner's arrival, this monument must have

been included among the works Langhans took Weinbrenner to see.

At the urging of the archaeologically inclined Genelli, Weinbrenner elected to continue his studies not in revolutionary Paris but in Rome, where he arrived in 1792. In the absence of a national German capital, Rome had served as a forum for intellectual discourse among Germans since Winckelmann's prolonged stay at mid-century and Goethe's visit in the 1780s. Weinbrenner's associates there included the luminaries of the German colony; among them were his traveling companions, the painter Asmus Jacob Carstens, the archaeologist and theorist Aloys Hirt, and the philosopher of esthetics Carl Ludwig Fernow. As in Berlin, the rediscovery of ancient Greek architecture galvanized the circle that gathered at the Café Greco.

The theoretical dilemma that motivated much of Weinbrenner's work in Rome and Italy was the question of the classical orders and their proportions. Weinbrenner was thus caught in the same tempest that had battered Claude Perrault over a century earlier. Just as Perrault had been confronted with discrepancies between the proportions of the orders as codified by Vitruvius and as displayed by ancient Roman buildings, Weinbrenner's generation was likewise confronted with the vast differences between the ancient Roman and ancient Greek orders. He and his contemporaries understood that there had to be rules. Yet if architectural beauty could no longer be based on a canon of fixed proportions, what rules should prevail?

For Weinbrenner this was a taxing question; having twice visited Paestum, he could no longer accept the constraints of the traditional view of the orders. With the image of baseless Doric columns still in mind, he condemned the "too strict adherence to the orders of Scamozzi, Vignola and Palladio" and railed against the "unconditional imitation of antiquity."[6] What is most significant is Weinbrenner's conviction, won in Italy, that the orders were not the carriers of architectural beauty:

Doubtless it was the authority of Vitruvius which spawned the error of regarding the columns as existing for their own sake and as predominant in architecture, without venturing to consider that they can only be parts—and usually only subordinate parts of a whole.[7]

For Weinbrenner beauty lay not in the ideal proportions of the orders; it was created when a building expressed its true character.

The term *caractère* had entered the architectural debate by 1780, when French architect Nicolas Le Camus de Mézières published *Le Genie de l'architecture*. Le Camus's best-known design, the Halle au blé in Paris, reflects the liberating influence of a doctrine holding that buildings could dramatize their function by unconventional but expressive forms. His book was rapidly translated into German, appearing in 1782 in *Huths Magazin der Bürgerlichen Baukunst*. By the 1790s a general appreciation of the role of character was part of the background of architectural thought in Germany, and even a general reference work such as C. L. Stieglitz's *Encyklopädie der Bürgerlichen Baukunst* (1792–98) offered a thorough discussion of the term. Like late eighteenth-century English associational theory, Stieglitz's view was that architectural proportions, textures, and ornament should arouse the viewer's emotions: Prisons should be designed to communicate feelings of dread, and gatehouses should inspire feelings of "masculine earnestness."[8]

This thinking shaped Weinbrenner's understanding of character and of the "characteristic" (*das Charakteristische*), but he sought a richer meaning for the term than the relatively straightforward model presented by Stieglitz. Borrowing from the more sophisticated work of contemporary German esthetic philosophers, he developed a dual definition of character that related it to the expression of either function or structure. In this, Weinbrenner was deeply indebted to Carl Ludwig Fernow (1763–1808), an exponent of Kant who had introduced that philosopher's ideas to Weinbrenner's circle in Rome.[9]

Fernow viewed character as the foundation of beauty, but he followed Kant in distinguishing between two kinds of beauty: one in which the ideal form of an object was determined by its fulfillment of a particular function and another that lacked such ideal forms. The latter class of objects—such as trees, rocks, or even human faces—had functions that did not demand an invariable formal solution; variations within the type neither impaired nor aided the fulfillment of that function.[10] Weinbrenner made much of this distinction, dividing architecture into two similar categories.

Weinbrenner included most of his work in a category of utilitarian buildings, which corresponded with Fernow's first class. These buildings were not civic or monumental. According to Fernow, the character of such structures must be the product of their purpose, and Weinbrenner concurred:

> The exterior of a building should suggest, as much as possible, its designation and interior function. The distinguishing features of its exterior, in accord with the interior, express most expediently and most directly the characteristic [*das Charakteristische*] of a building.[11]

However, for designs of a nobler caste like churches or palaces (akin to Fernow's second class), character lay not in the perfect expression of function. The character of such buildings depended in part on the use of the traditional vocabulary of classical architecture and in the contrivance of general contours and proportions. Most important, Weinbrenner argued that the system of construction determined the physiognomy of buildings in this category. This could be as distinctive as the physiognomy of the human face, he averred, borrowing his vocabulary directly from Fernow:

> The construction of a building is to an architect what the skeletal and muscular system is to a painter or sculptor. These are only the inner parts of the whole, but through form and contour they give the exterior its essential character.[12]

The overt materialism of Weinbrenner's analysis of this second category of architecture ran directly contrary to the kind of classical idealism that was espoused by other members of the Café Greco coterie. For example, the archaeologist Aloys Hirt (1759–1837) still believed that classical Greek architecture was the lithification of earlier wooden forms. Hirt's interpretation rested on the authority of tradition and assumed the subordination of materials to ideal forms. His was a fundamentally conservative outlook holding that if the ancient Greeks had been faithful to the architectural forms of their predecessors, then so also should the architects of Hirt's generation be faithful to the forms of the classical tradition.

While Weinbrenner drew the illustrations for Hirt's *Die Baukunst nach den Grundsätzen der Alten* (published in 1809 but already begun in Rome during the 1790s), he could not have been satisfied with a model that ignored the essential differences between wood and masonry construction. Indeed, he ultimately retorted that wooden forms could only be translated into stone when stone was used as a protective mantel over wooden structural elements. In all other cases, the "artistic-static" properties of stone required a fully distinct set of proportions.[13] Weinbrenner explained:

> According to the ancient Greek and Roman orders one would assume that the beauty of the columns should be sought in the correct proportions of the separate parts without regard for the material; but when one imagines a column shaft of the same height and width of stone, wood and iron, supporting an equally great load, it defies healthy human reason if we make the iron as thick as the wood, or the wood as thick as the stone.[14]

Not only proportion, but form and contour as well, were related to the choice of material. Once again, Weinbrenner turned to wood architecture for instruction:

> If one assumes that beauty rests solely in the naked form, then the materials do not come into considera-

tion. But because the materials must coexist in a harmonious union with the perfected object, we are always stirred by an unpleasant feeling . . . when we see the outlines . . . contradicting the natural properties of the material. So, for example, the form of a round ball of wood, where the contours of the form cut perpendicularly across the grain of the wood, causes displeasure which we would not perceive in another material.[15]

It is significant that Weinbrenner, a trained carpenter, should have used his understanding of wood joinery as the foundation of his critique of classical idealism. In this respect his analysis was a characteristic German phenomenon, distinct and detached from the French academic tradition. It derived from the fact that stuccoed brick and stuccoed half-timbering remained in Weinbrenner's day the principal German construction materials, even for major public buildings. Ashlar masonry was far less common than in France, where civic architecture was stone architecture, a state of affairs confirmed by French architectural education and its emphasis on stone construction. Such a focus would have been misplaced in Germany, and a view of architectural history that neglected wood building was troubling to Weinbrenner, who wrote:

> Because stone construction has been researched and developed more than wood construction, beginning with the revival of architecture in the Middle Ages and extending to the present day, we are spurred on to render special study to wood construction, based on the appropriate use of wood and on the natural laws of beauty, so that it may be used in higher architecture to the same degree as it was in classical antiquity.[16]

As an example of the principles of wood construction, Weinbrenner called attention to the buildings he designed for Prince Putiatin around 1794 (cat. 20).

It is not surprising that in the 1790s David Gilly had also turned to wood construction as a fertile source of architectural form, using wooden structural systems to create unconventional, boldly contoured buildings. In his *Ueber die Erfindung, Con-*

struction und Vortheile der Bohlen-Dächer (1797), Gilly argued for a revival of curved beamed roofs, a medieval form. Like Weinbrenner, he tapped the forms and techniques of Germany's vernacular tradition to enrich the classical language; in doing so he helped to reconcile the classical heritage and Germany's wooden legacy. Although Weinbrenner admired the structural acumen of these roofs, he rejected Gilly's innovation on the firmly materialist ground that the artificial curving of wood beams violated the natural properties of the material.[17]

IN 1798, Weinbrenner began his career in Karlsruhe with the design of a synagogue (cat. 50). Composed of several discrete architectural motifs from widely dispersed historical eras and brought together with no attempt to integrate them into a conventional stylistic whole, the synagogue is the most striking example of the liberating effects of Weinbrenner's theory of architectural character from the constraints of idealism. Heinrich Gentz (1766–1811), whom Weinbrenner would have known from their overlapping periods of study in Rome, described his own Berlin Mint, likewise begun in 1798, with words that could be applied to Weinbrenner's design:

> I have heard that there have been disputes over the style in which this building has been executed; whether in Roman, or in Greek, or in Egyptian taste? To this I reply that I imagined neither a Roman, nor a Greek, nor an Egyptian ideal during the composition process, rather, that I first vigorously filled my spirit with the purpose of the building and then designed a facade which was not only appropriate to the whole, but which was necessarily derived from it.[18]

Few other Weinbrenner designs depart so radically from convention, although medieval forms detached from their context appear in the towers of Karlsruhe's Rathaus and Catholic church. Similarly, there is little trace of the nearly radical materialism of Weinbrenner's written theory in the stuccoed edifices that comprise most of his work. It was principally in the work of his students that these ideas were given substance.

In the fullness of time, the seed of Weinbrenner's ahistorical materialism yielded rich fruit. In 1828 his student Heinrich Hübsch described a new architectural style in his famous *In welchem Style sollen wir bauen?*, proclaiming that architectural form, as in Weinbrenner's physiognomic model, depended upon construction. The individual details of Rundbogenstil buildings, Hübsch said, could be left to the architect's "free fantasy," rendering the ancient authorities meaningless.[19]

The actual forms of the Rundbogenstil, like its philosophy, resulted from Weinbrenner's investigations. Its round arches with profiled archivolts, polychromatic voussoirs, pilaster strips, corbel tables, and gable-capped pavilions were derived from the German medieval forms—chiefly Romanesque—that Weinbrenner and his students had explored (cats. 81–84). Assisted by Hübsch and Georg Moller, Weinbrenner helped to root Germany's modern architecture in her indigenous medieval heritage, still flourishing in the building practices of German craftsmen in Weinbrenner's day. They recognized that Germany's relative poverty in classical ruins did not deprive her of a worthy historical tradition.

Weinbrenner's most lasting effect was therefore not to be found in the neoclassical forms with which he transformed Karlsruhe, for these had fallen into disfavor within a few years of his death. It rested instead on his contribution to the establishment of a German academic and architectural tradition, based in large part on a materialist definition of architectural character and bound up inextricably with native building practices. Weinbrenner's ideas divide the eighteenth from the nineteenth century, separating forever classical idealists like Aloys Hirt and scholars like Karl Bötticher, whose *Die Tektonik der Hellenen* (1844) sought to explain Greek architecture—in terms Weinbrenner would have understood—according to the timeless laws of tectonics and structure.

NOTES

1. For a discussion of the role of regionalism during this period, see Werner Oechslin, "Zur Architektur des Klassizismus in Deutschland," in *Klassizismus in Bayern, Schwaben und Franken*, ed. Winfried Nerdinger (Munich: Munich Stadtmuseum, 1980), 1–14.

2. Legeay did not achieve an instant transformation of Berlin architecture. For a discussion of a mini-baroque revival following his departure, see Fritz Landesberger, *Die Kunst der Goethezeit* (Leipzig: Im Insel-Verlag, 1931).

3. Weinbrenner (1958, 31).

4. Ibid.

5. The antipathy Weinbrenner's writings often exhibited toward French architecture may date from this period, when he discovered the "purity" of Berlin architecture at the expense of the "affectations" of French taste; see Weinbrenner (1926, 3, 40).

6. Ibid., 6–7.

7. Ibid., 7.

8. C. L. Stieglitz, *Encyklopädie der Bürgerlichen Baukunst*, 5 vols. (Leipzig: C. Fritsch, 1792–98).

9. Fernow's aesthetic theory was to have been codified in his *Ästhetisches Handbuch für bildende Künstler*, which he prepared during the winter of 1795–96 when he was in frequent contact with Weinbrenner and when they projected a joint publication on Sicily (see Weinbrenner [1958, 196, 210]). For Fernow, see Irmgard Fernow, *Carl Ludwig Fernow als Ästhetiker: Ein Vergleich mit der "Kritik der Urteilskraft"* (Würzburg: Richard Mayer, 1936).

10. Fernow, op. cit., 27, 32–33.

11. Ibid., 69.

12. Ibid., 3. Weinbrenner was not alone in his physiognomic definition of character; Schinkel used physiognomy as a synonym for character in his unpublished *Lehrbuch*; see Goerd Peschken, *Karl Friedrich Schinkel Lebenswerk: Das architektonische Lehrbuch* (Munich and Berlin: Deutscher Kunstverlag, 1979), 22.

13. Weinbrenner, (1926, 7).

14. Ibid., 13–14.

15. Ibid., 13.

16. Weinbrenner, "Die Villa des Fürsten Putiatin in Schackwitz," [Leipziger] *Abendzeitung* no. 151 (June 1817).

17. Weinbrenner (1926, 5). For buildings in and around Berlin with curved beamed ceilings, see David Gilly, *Ueber die Erfindung, Construction und Vortheile der Bohlen-Dächer* (Berlin: F. Vieweg, 1797).

18. Adolph Doebber, *Heinrich Gentz: Ein Berliner Baumeister um 1800* (Berlin: Carl Heymann, 1916), 45.

19. For Hübsch's challenge to Hirt, see Barry Bergdoll, "Archaeology vs. History: Heinrich Hübsch's Critique of Neoclassicism and the Beginnings of Historicism in German Architectural History," *Oxford Art Journal* 5 (1981–82): 3–12.

Catalogue of
Selected Drawings

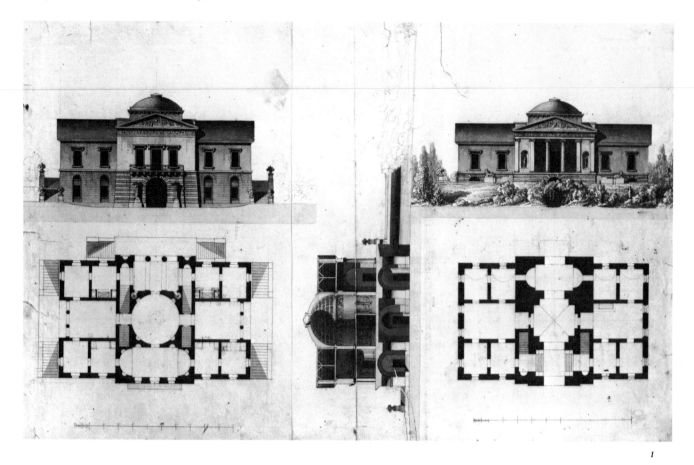

1

1–3 (2.1, 2.2, 2.4v)
VILLA AND ESTATE OF
MARGRAVINE CHRISTIANE
LOUISE, KARLSRUHE
Friedrich Weinbrenner, architect

Weinbrenner's lifelong fascination with Palladianism found its fullest realization in this variation on the Villa Rotunda, built for one of the daughters-in-law of Grand Duke Karl Friedrich. Arranged with a dozen smaller buildings in a naturalistic park in the southwest quarter of the city, the house bespoke that mixture of English taste and French fashion that infused German architecture at the outset of the nineteenth century (see fig. 3).

Karl Friedrich had given his second son, Margrave Friedrich, the garden site in 1804. Friedrich often discussed the possibilities of the estate with Weinbrenner, and he employed the architect to rebuild the castle at Neu-Eberstein in 1803 and 1804 (checklist 96.1–96.3) and to convert the von Beck, Jöslin, and Reutlinger houses into one great residence on the Schloss Strasse in 1809 (cat. 37). However, he died on May 28, 1817, before plans for this villa were approved. His widow Christiane Louise then became

the patron, dedicating the project to her husband's memory, and early in August 1817 she directed Weinbrenner to prepare a definitive design. On August 15 she approved plans for the villa, and on August 29, the late margrave's sixty-first birthday, the cornerstone was laid. Weinbrenner was able to prepare the design so rapidly because of at least a decade of preliminary discussion, but construction was slow and the decoration of the building was still incomplete when the architect died in 1826.

The first two drawings (cats. 1, 2), probably the work of assistants, show

2

the villa in its garden. Weinbrenner's Palladianism was modernized by the placement of the building atop a mysterious, grotto-like passage (in fact contrived to allow visitors to quit their carriages in shelter). This romantic imagery recalled recent French architecture, like Claude-Nicolas Ledoux's Hôtel Thelusson in Paris (1778–81), erected over a similar grotto.

The basement level of the villa (cat. 1, lower right) contained the entrance passage, the kitchen, and servants' rooms. The main floor (cat. 1, lower left) centered on the great circular sa-lon, adjacent to the apse-ended dining room. The small bedrooms are identi-fied by their bed alcoves. In the final version of this design, tiny servant stairs connected some of these sleep-ing rooms with the basement; their absence here suggests that these are early drawings, perhaps from 1817.

The sculptural program indicated in these drawings was never executed. It includes representations of Mother Nature feeding the animals in the west tympanum (cat. 2) and Apollo with the muses in the south pediment (cat. 1, top right). The celebrated benefac-tions of the late margrave were to fill the north pediment (cat. 1, top left). Friedrich was an army officer in Dutch service, but he was an eccentric who spent little time with his troops. He was best known in Karlsruhe as the art patron and philanthropist who gave bread to the poor during the bleak winter of 1816–17.

The villa is sketched atop its ar-tificial hill in a third drawing (cat. 3); to the right stands the garden house (cat. 4), and to the left the tiny Ionic temple that sheltered a bust of Mar-grave Friedrich. Weinbrenner's role in designing the garden is not certain; the work was executed under the di-

3

rection of Andreas Hartweg, the court gardener. The other side of this sheet (not illustrated) shows a north elevation of the villa, apparently made in preparation for the 1822 volume of Weinbrenner's *Ausgeführte und projectirte Gebäude*.

Not visible in any of these drawings is the railing that circled the villa's dome, creating there an extraordinary belvedere. On summer evenings, Weinbrenner wrote, the rooftop afforded a "delightful . . . view of the departing sun as it hides itself behind the Vosges, while the mountain masses darken in the glowing golden sunset and the last rays of daylight still illumine the familiar peaks of the Black Forest hills."

The villa and most of the other buildings on the estate were demolished when Josef Durm built a palace for the crown grand duke on this site between 1891 and 1897. That building now serves as the Supreme Court of the Federal Republic of Germany. *D. B.*

BIBLIOGRAPHY

Everke 1981, 57–58; Geier n.d.; Lankheit 1976, 17–25, 39–40, 18 and 19 (ills.); *Sammlung* 1847–58, 51; Schumacher c. 1850, 163r–166r; Valdenaire 1919 (2d ed., 1926, 155–59); Weinbrenner 1822–35 (reprint, 1978, vol. 1, and Kommentar, 3–5, 4 [ill.]).

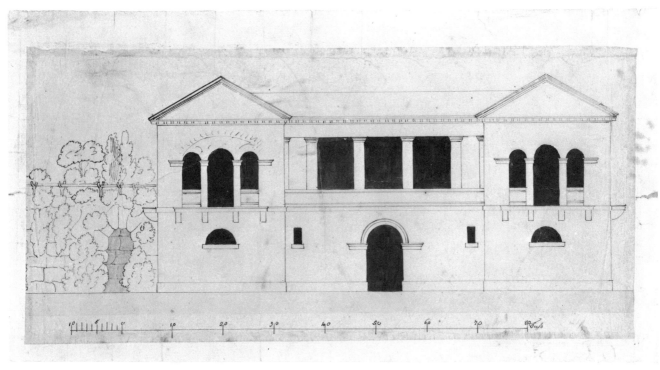

4

4 (2.10)

MARGRAVINE CHRISTIANE LOUISE'S GARDEN HOUSE

Friedrich Weinbrenner, architect

For small-scale entertainment Weinbrenner built this garden house at the southwest corner of the estate. Reached from the main house by means of a rustic viaduct, the upper floor contained a dining room at center, flanked by a vestibule at left and the tiny apartment of a serving woman at right. The great windows of the dining salon allowed it to be filled with summer plants and afforded visitors an elevated view of the adjacent park and lake. The ground floor sheltered the estate's chickens, peacocks, swans, and ducks. This drawing is apparently a copy of one made when the building was constructed, c. 1817–18. *D. B.*

BIBLIOGRAPHY

Lankheit 1976, 18, 19 (ill.), 20–25, 39–40; Weinbrenner 1822–35 (reprint, 1978, vol. 1, 8).

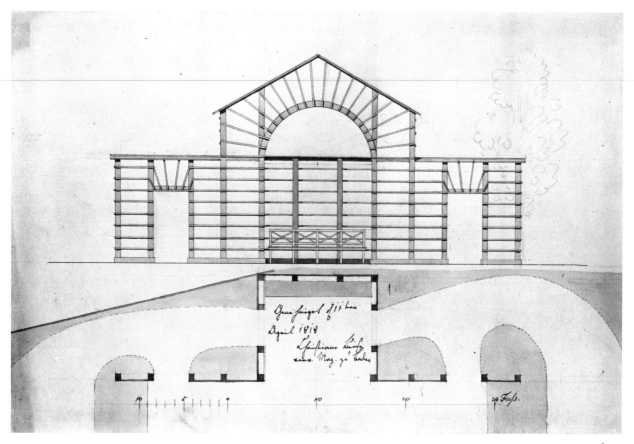

5

5 (2.14)
MARGRAVINE CHRISTIANE
LOUISE'S GARDEN ARBOR
Friedrich Weinbrenner, architect

The margravine herself signed this drawing, indicating her approval, on April 11, 1818. This and her similar signature on another drawing (cat. 7), two weeks earlier, suggest that Weinbrenner had devoted the winter of 1817–18 to the design of the smaller structures on the estate. He presented them to Christiane in the spring, and they were probably erected that summer.

The depicted trellis stood at the east end of the linden alley that ran from the main estate entrance (at the west in the Herrenstrasse) across the north end of the garden, passing in front of the plant house (cat. 6). Beyond the Herrenstrasse, the Amalienstrasse continued the line of the garden walk westward, and Weinbrenner noted: "From this leafy trellis one could, while unobserved, observe the Amalienstrasse and those who passed the principal gate of the garden." *D. B.*

BIBLIOGRAPHY

Lankheit 1976, 18–20, 20 (ill.), 39; Weinbrenner 1822–35 (reprint, 1978, vol. 1, 10 and Kommentar, 5).

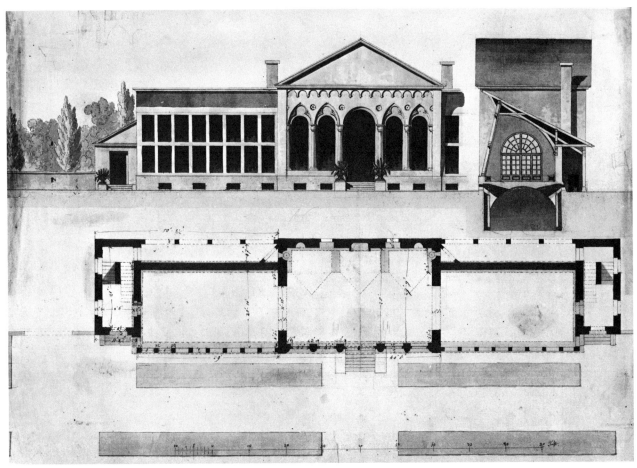

6

6 (2.12)
MARGRAVINE CHRISTIANE
LOUISE'S PLANT HOUSE
Friedrich Weinbrenner, architect

In the plant house at the north end of the garden, Weinbrenner permitted himself the license of a mongrel Gothic, with roundheaded windows set beneath pointed arches. While he fostered the taste for medieval architecture in his students, he used such forms sparingly in his own work. Less hardy plants were wintered in the central room of the building, the orangery, and this airy space could be used for entertainment in the summer. From its central, south-facing doorway, a visitor could spy the distant church tower in the village of Beiertheim, exactly framed by the passageway beneath the Palladian villa at the other end of the garden. The side wings of the plant house were used as cool and warm rooms for exotics, which required year-round protection. Vegetables were stored in the well-ventilated basement. *D. B.*

BIBLIOGRAPHY

Schumacher c. 1850, 48r; Staatliche Kunsthalle 1977, 132–33, 139 (ill.); Weinbrenner 1822–35 (reprint, 1978, vol. 1, 8–9 and Kommentar, 5).

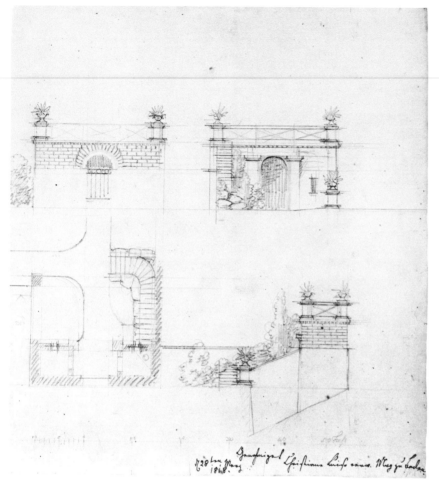

7

7 (2.13)
GATEWAY TO MARGRAVINE CHRISTIANE LOUISE'S VEGETABLE GARDEN
Friedrich Weinbrenner, architect

The margravine also owned a vegetable garden south of the Kriegsstrasse, laid out in formal parterres, for which Weinbrenner designed several small buildings. Two gatehouses at the Kriegsstrasse corners of the garden were built to this design, following its approval by Christiane Louise on March 28, 1818. On that date she affixed her signature at the lower right. The north boundary of the vegetable garden, like the south boundary of the main estate, was defined by a sunken fence or "ha-ha," which can be seen in the side elevation at lower right. This device allowed visitors to enjoy an uninterrupted view of the margravine's property, as though the Kriegsstrasse did not exist. Another view of the villa (cat. 3) was evidently sketched from a position among the tidy rows of vegetables that stood adjacent to this building. The structure contained a toilet and storeroom on either side of the archway, with an upper terrace where Weinbrenner suggested that seeds might be dried. *D. B.*

BIBLIOGRAPHY

Weinbrenner 1822–35 (reprint, 1978, vol. 1, 10 and Kommentar, 5).

8

8 (2.15)
MARGRAVINE CHRISTIANE LOUISE'S STABLE AND GARDENER'S HOUSE
Friedrich Weinbrenner, architect

The great portal of this utilitarian structure opened in the Herrenstrasse just north of the main gate of the estate, giving access to the stable yard behind. The ground floor accommodated horse stalls and a coal storeroom to the left, while the head gardener was quartered to the right, with a tiny paymaster's office in the front corner. The master of the margravine's household occupied the apartment on the upper floor. Respecting the conventions established by the abutting houses, the stuccoed street facade imitated rusticated masonry in its lower story. For the side elevation Weinbrenner prepared a more challenging design dominated by his favorite Palladian borrowing: a pediment invaded by a thermal window like that at the Villa Foscari. Although altered, the gardener's house still stands, the sole survivor of Weinbrenner's works for Christiane Louise. *D. B.*

BIBLIOGRAPHY

Weinbrenner 1822–35 (reprint, 1978, vol. 1, 9).

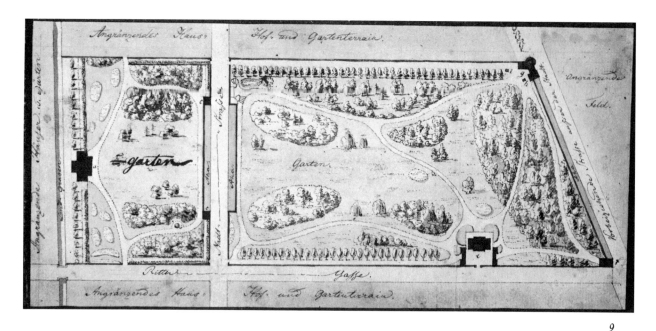

9

9, 10 (4.1, 4.2)
VILLA AND ESTATE OF MARGRAVINE AMALIE, KARLSRUHE
Friedrich Weinbrenner, architect

Just east of the estate of Margravine Christiane Louise (cats. 1–8) lay the smaller villa and garden of her sister-in-law Amalie (1754–1832), the wife of Karl Friedrich's eldest son and heir apparent, Crown Prince Karl Ludwig. Here, work had begun earlier, and while the budget was smaller, the ensemble of buildings was by no means less remarkable.

Amalie and Karl Ludwig had married in 1774, and they lived at first with the groom's father in the towered palace at the center of Karlsruhe's circular plan. However, perhaps to escape the company of Karl Friedrich's young second wife, they built a summerhouse in 1787 and 1788 in the crown prince's small garden north of the Erbprinzenstrasse. This Palladian building, designed by Wilhelm Jeremias Müller, appears at left in cat. 9 (in which the Erbprinzenstrasse is labeled "Stadt Strasse" and north is to the left). At the same time they engaged Friedrich Schweikardt, the court gardener, to redesign the grounds in the English style.

In 1800 the royal couple began to discuss a new house with Weinbrenner, then just returned from his long years of student travel, and, with acquisition of the much larger parcel of ground south of the Erbprinzenstrasse, the serious planning started. The location for the new villa on the Ritterstrasse was selected by June 1801, and Weinbrenner set to work on the final design, hoping to have it ready for presentation when the couple returned from their fall and winter trip to Saint Petersburg and Stockholm, where they would visit their daughters, the czarina of Russia and the queen of Sweden.

Sadly, the crown prince died in a carriage accident in Sweden on December 16, 1801, and it was left to his grieving father to see that the buildings were completed as a memorial to his son and as a home for his widowed daughter-in-law. Rejecting Weinbrenner's first and larger neo-Palladian villa design because of the cost of its dome and portico, he selected an alternative version (cat. 10). In this the architect attached a tower like those he had admired in the farmhouses of Italy to a simplified composition of house and forecourt. The strikingly autonomous geometry of the design bears comparison with the work of French romantic classicists. When Amalie at last returned from Sweden in May 1802, she found the house nearly completed; the other new buildings on the estate were readied within the next year.

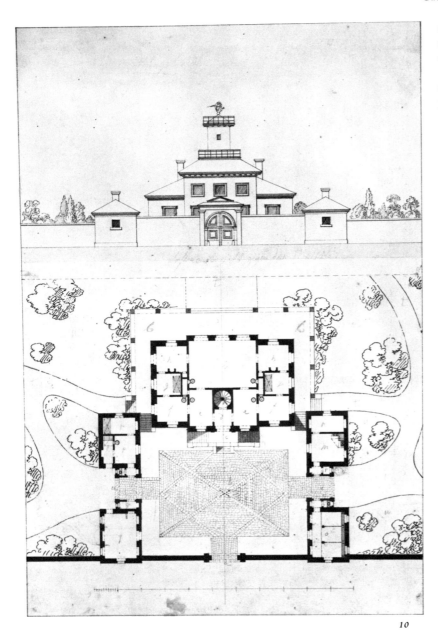

10

court included the kitchen and stable at right and the gardener's house and quarters for male servants at left.

Design of the enlarged garden was entrusted to Friedrich Schweikardt. To preserve the splendid views of the distant Black Forest from the old summerhouse, he left the central area as an open lawn, punctuated by clumped trees in the English fashion. The encroachment of the Erbprinzenstrasse was minimized by the use of ha-has rather than obstructive walls, and a tunnel beneath the road, lined with memorials to the margravine's departed friends, connected the two parts of the estate.

In the southwest corner of the garden (lower right in cat. 10), Weinbrenner built an aviary, while the southeast corner was occupied by his very substantial Gothic tower. The latter contained a chapel dedicated to the memory of Karl Ludwig, and its medieval forms were presumably chosen for their relevance to this sacred function. However, the building also contained a splendid bath.

Müller's villa was demolished in 1865, followed by the Gothic tower in 1867, and the aviary was moved to the garden of the Grand Ducal Palace in 1884. The house designed by Weinbrenner survived, used for a variety of educational, social service, and museum functions, but on September 26, 1944, it fell victim to Allied bombing. Its foundations stand today in a small park called the Nymphengarten. *D. B.*

BIBLIOGRAPHY

Everke 1981, 54–56; Hirsch 1928–32, vol. 2, 40–66; *Sammlung* 1847–58, 48; Schumacher c. 1850, 168r–170r; Valdenaire 1919 (2d ed., 1926, 159–60); Weinbrenner 1822–35 (reprint 1978, vol. 2 and Kommentar, 5–8).

The little villa provided only relatively simple living quarters, and Müller's old summerhouse was preserved to accommodate large parties. Two bedroom suites (one was intended for the late crown prince) flanked the entrance on the ground floor, with a two-story dining room and adjoining work rooms facing the garden. The low service buildings framing the

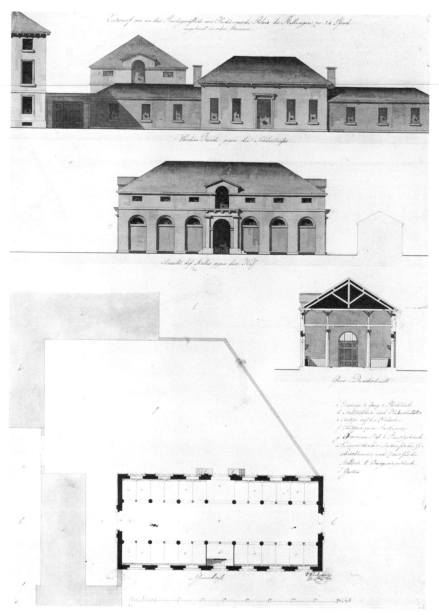

11

11 (6.6)
STABLE ADDITION FOR THE MARGRAVES' PALACE, KARLSRUHE
Friedrich Weinbrenner, architect

For the three sons borne by his second wife, Grand Duke Karl Friedrich built a great Palladian town house on the Rondellplatz, with gardens stretching behind it to the Kriegsstrasse (see fig. 2). One of young Weinbrenner's first commissions, the planning of this palace for Margraves Leopold (grand duke, 1830–52), Wilhelm, and Maximilian began in 1799, and construction started in 1803. The palace's first service building (elevation at top) was built in the Schloss Strasse in 1809; its central block was an orangery, with tack rooms and accommodations for stablehands in the wings. By 1814 the sober stable detailed in the center and bottom of this autographed drawing had been erected.

The austere geometry of the new building, with its enwrapping blind arcade, bespoke the revolutionary sensibilities of the era around 1800. Save for the Doric doorway, there was almost no external enrichment, but the hayloft and roof structure were supported by two interior rows of Ionic columns. The stable survived the Second World War but was later demolished. *D. B.*

BIBLIOGRAPHY

Lankheit 1976, 43 (ill.), 49, 50; Schumacher c. 1850, 49r; Valdenaire 1919 (2d ed., 1926, 147).

12

12–14 (6.2, 6.3, 6.5)
MARGRAVES' GARDEN HOUSE, KARLSRUHE
Friedrich Weinbrenner, architect

While awaiting the completion of the Margraves' Palace, the grand ducal household made use of a garden house that Weinbrenner built against the south, Kriegsstrasse wall of the estate between 1800 and 1804. The building provided rudimentary overnight accommodation and spectacular views of the adjacent countryside.

The collection preserves several of the architect's preliminary designs for this commission, many recorded in later copies by one of Weinbrenner's finest draftsmen, Ferdinand Thierry (see also checklist 6.1, 6.4). Two drawings (cats. 12, 13) show a proposal for a dignified temple-fronted structure, with a splendid central hall and a small bedroom tucked in the right wing. The ambitious Pompeian-colored wall paintings depict ancient maidens dancing with garlands. This small, rich design was surely inspired by the debating room whose decoration had been described by Lucian in the second century. In "The Hall," Lucian had praised "the refined symmetry of its gilding, which is not unnecessarily lavish, but only in such degree as would suffice a modest and beautiful woman to set off her beauty." Weinbrenner had drawn a reconstruction of this jewel-like structure while in Rome in the 1790s, which he finally published in 1822.

The third drawing (cat. 14) shows the garden house almost as it was erected, although the actual building had Ionic columns. Apparently recognizing that the construction of the palace would require at least a decade,

Karl Friedrich authorized the construction of this more ambitious garden house to serve in the interim. A miniature version of Palladio's domed Villa Rotunda, it prefigured Weinbrenner's later house for Margravine Christiane Louise (cats. 1, 2). The drawing also shows the rooftop walkway that Weinbrenner added in order to exploit the views toward Durlach in the east. The garden house stood until 1902. *D. B.*

BIBLIOGRAPHY

Everke 1981, 53–54; Geier n.d.; Lankheit 1976, 15 (ill.), 20–25, 22 (ill.), 39, 40; *Lucian*, trans. A. M. Harmon (London: William Heinemann, 1913), vol. 1, 183–85; Schumacher c. 1850, 65; Valdenaire 1919 (2d ed., 1926, 139–41); Weinbrenner 1822–34, vol. 1, 3–15; Weinbrenner 1822–35 (reprint, 1978, Kommentar, 6).

14

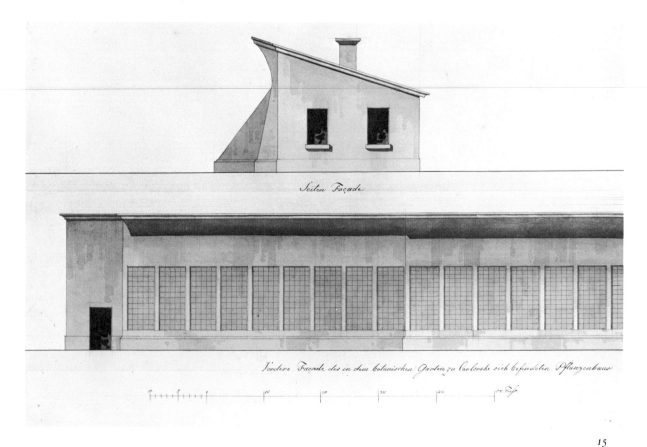

Seiten Façade

Vordere Façade des in dem botanischen Garten zu Carlsruhe sich befindelen Pflanzenhaus

15

15 (34.1)
PLANT HOUSE, BOTANICAL GARDEN, KARLSRUHE
Friedrich Weinbrenner, architect

Grand Duke Karl Friedrich was an avid gardener, with both esthetic and scientific interest in the subject. Under his direction the landscape architect Friedrich Schweikardt remade the formal, French-style palace gardens according to English principles, and, in the first decade of the nineteenth century, Weinbrenner began building for him a great complex of greenhouses and orangeries west of the palace. The latter work complemented the increasingly scientific approach to agriculture in Baden (see cats. 28–34).

In 1807 Weinbrenner presented an imposing first design, centered on a domed winter garden and including a house for the court botanist and two smaller greenhouses. This was judged too costly, and the plans were revised. An old orangery was allowed to remain in use, the proposed dome was eliminated, and the new buildings were generally simplified. This drawing shows the simplest auxiliary greenhouse as executed, with its inclined roof reaching upward to expose the raking, south-facing windows. Weinbrenner's buildings in this garden were built slowly between 1808 and 1824; between 1853 and 1857 they were demolished when Heinrich Hübsch rebuilt the complex. *D. B.*

BIBLIOGRAPHY

Gutman 1911, 94; Schirmer 1977, 134–39, 285; Schumacher c. 1850, 210r–211r; Städtische Galerie 1983, 96–97; Tschira 1939, 109–17; Valdenaire 1919 (2d ed., 1926, 120).

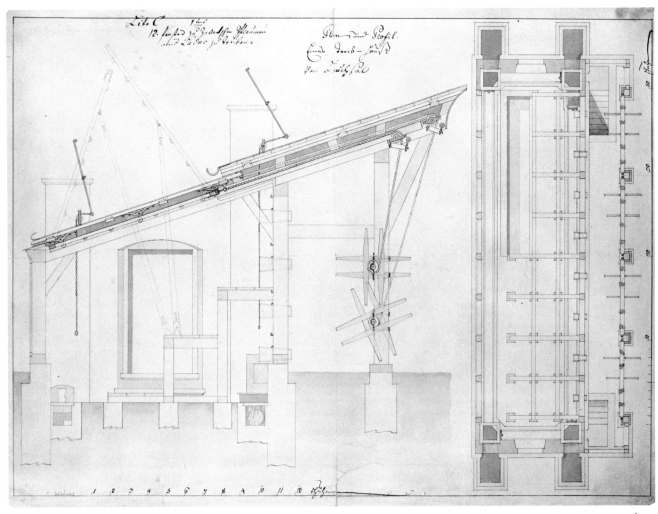

16

16 (36.1)
PLANT HOUSE, BRUCHSAL
Friedrich Weinbrenner, architect

Margravine Amalie, the widow of Crown Prince Karl Ludwig, soon abandoned the Karlsruhe villa built for her by Weinbrenner (see cats. 9, 10) and took up residence in the beautiful rococo palace at Bruchsal, the former seat of the bishop of Speyer.

This drawing shows the plan (right) and operating details (left) of a greenhouse for her fruit trees. The design was probably produced in Weinbrenner's office soon after the turn of the century.

Unlike the plant house in the Karlsruhe botanical garden (cat. 15), the Bruchsal building had a glass roof. Its panels (pink in section) could be hinged upward from top or bottom,

or fully retracted, to provide ventilation. Shutters (yellow in section) could be winched down to cover the glass and keep out the sun. A modern road and rail line cross the estate where the greenhouse once stood.
D. B.

BIBLIOGRAPHY

Hirsch 1906, 71–72; Rott 1913, 118.

17

17 (32.1)
RUINED GARDEN TEMPLE, KARLSRUHE (?)
Friedrich Weinbrenner or Miessel, architect (?)

Under the patronage of Grand Duke Karl Friedrich and his children, the taste for English gardening flourished in Baden well into the nineteenth century. Picturesque parks were filled with scores of small, fanciful structures like this temple, a constructed ruin, whose crumbling pediment has been converted by nature into a garden. Inside stands a tomb, a melancholy reminder that the building's decay foreshadows the fate of man. This structure does not closely resemble the ruin that stood in the palace's pheasantry garden, which had a different plan. Like many other unidentified garden buildings in the collection, it may be a design prepared during the thirteen years of planning that preceded the construction of Margravine Christiane Louise's estate in 1817 (cats. 1–8). Nothing is known of the draftsman Miessel, who probably came from Weinbrenner's office.
D. B.

BIBLIOGRAPHY

Berendt 1926, 44.

18

18 (18.1)
ROMAN HOUSE, ROTENFELS
Friedrich Weinbrenner, architect

This proud design atop a hill is a preliminary project for the so-called
Roman house that Weinbrenner built
in 1808 at Rotenfels. It was placed on
the grounds of the earthenware factory established there by Grand
Duchess Luise Caroline, Karl Friedrich's second wife. The classical allu-
sion in the name suggests that it was
conceived under the anti-urban spell
cast by Latin poets like Virgil and
Theocritus. Although the superstruc-
ture of the building was destroyed in
1899, its foundations (incorporating
parts of earlier construction on the
site) still stand on a now densely
wooded hillside. Below lies the country house Weinbrenner built at
Rotenfels between 1818 and 1827 for
the grand duchess's son, Margrave
Wilhelm von Hochberg, and beyond
stretches the Murg Valley, broadening
about twenty kilometers south of
Karlsruhe as it meets the Rhine plain.
D. B.

BIBLIOGRAPHY

Hirschfeld 1963, 330–33; Schumacher
c. 1850, 184r; Valdenaire 1919 (2d ed.,
1926, 171–73).

19

19 (26.1)
GARDENER'S HOUSE WITH BRIDGE
School of Weinbrenner (Miessel?)

Reached by crossing a disintegrating arch, this rustic gardener's cottage was designed for a site like that of the garden house in Margravine Christiane Louise's estate, built c. 1817–18 (cat. 4). It may be a preliminary project for that building. The drawing style recalls the elevation of a ruined temple signed by Miessel (cat. 17). *D. B.*

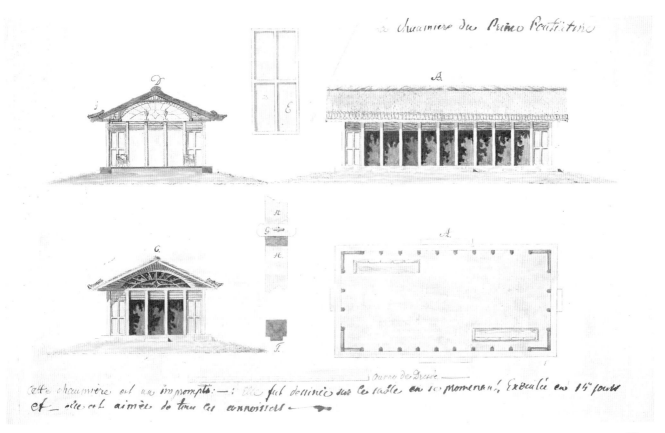

20

20 (24.1)
THATCHED PAVILION FOR PRINCE PUTIATIN, SCHACKWITZ
Friedrich Weinbrenner, architect

Drawn on English paper with a 1794 watermark, this charming wooden entertainment pavilion is the earliest work by Weinbrenner of which a representation survives. The building's story and a glimpse of aristocratic life around 1800 are contained in the long French inscription (This thatched cabin is an impromptu: It was designed in ten seconds at the table! Built in fifteen days and loved by all the connoisseurs). The client, Prince Nikolai Putiatin (1744–1818), was a Russian courtier who commissioned several wooden buildings from Weinbrenner for his estate at Schackwitz, near Dresden. Weinbrenner apparently met Putiatin in 1791, when he visited Dresden briefly, and this design must have been sent north a few years later from Rome, where Weinbrenner was then studying. The buildings at Schackwitz were the subject of a newspaper article by Weinbrenner in 1817, in which he extolled the virtues of wood construction and hailed its longevity. *D. B.*

BIBLIOGRAPHY

Friedrich Weinbrenner, "Die Villa des Fürsten Putiatin in Schackwitz," [Leipziger] *Abendzeitung* no. 151 (25 June 1817).

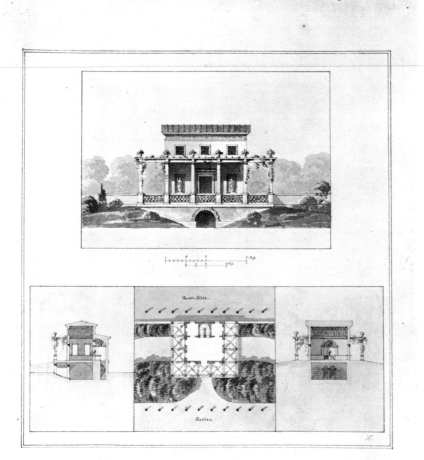

21

21 (8.1)
GARDEN HOUSE WITH ARBOR,
QUERALLEE, KARLSRUHE
School of Weinbrenner

An exquisite structure, this little garden house is identified by inscriptions on the verso. It was evidently planned for the grounds of one of the early nineteenth-century houses built along the east arm of the Lange Strasse; the gardens of houses south of that major thoroughfare ran southward to the Querallee, where this building was to stand. Since the Querallee was renamed Zähringerstrasse in 1809, a terminus ante quem is provided for this design.

The exceptional cubic clarity of the conceit suggests that its author was familiar with such French-inspired garden architecture as he could have seen in the *Ideenmagazin für Liebhaber von Gärten* (1796–1811) or the *Taschenbuch für Natur- und Gartenfreunde* (1795–1806) (see checklist 42.1–42.6). The monogram (Ж) at lower right has not been identified, but the work almost surely comes from Weinbrenner's circle. *D. B.*

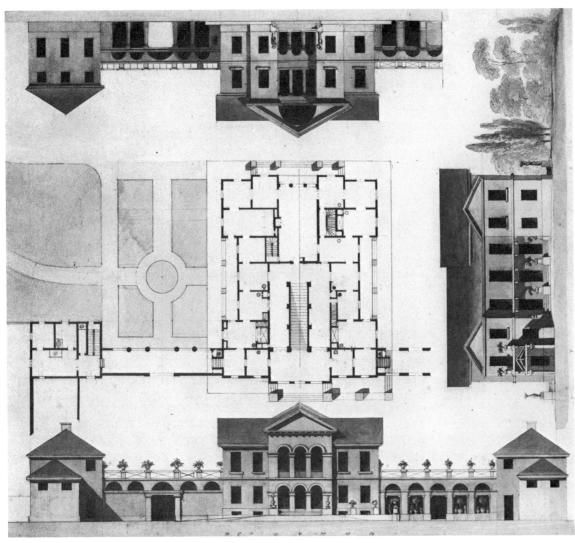

22

22 (86.1)
SUMMER PALACE FOR QUEEN FRIEDERIKE OF SWEDEN (?), BADEN-BADEN
Friedrich Weinbrenner, architect

Friederike of Baden, daughter of Crown Prince Karl Ludwig and Margravine Amalie (see cats. 9, 10), married King Gustav Adolphus IV of Sweden in 1797. When the king abdicated in 1809 and divorced her Friederike returned home, remodeling a summer palace in Baden-Baden to Weinbrenner's design in 1821. Although much altered, her home still stands in the famous spa town, at that end of the fashionable Lichtentaler Allee closest to Weinbrenner's Kurhaus.

The executed building, whose completion required many years, incorporated an old structure and comprised two wings of different heights. This drawing shares certain facade features with the actual building and may be an ideal project for an entirely new and symmetrical palace. The ter-

22 (detail)

rain, however, does not resemble the site of the present structure, and this design may have been intended for another client. The work is Palladian in its orderly concatenation of service buildings, and the rear elevation (top) exhibits Weinbrenner's favorite borrowing from the Vicentine master, a pediment broken by a large thermal window. The same motif was favored by Ledoux, and the general sparseness of detail and geometrical clarity reflect Weinbrenner's admiration for recent French design.

The colorful drawing, with its lively depiction of foliage, may be the work of Ferdinand Thierry (see cats. 25–27). *D. B.*

BIBLIOGRAPHY

Lacroix et al. 1942, 345; Lankheit 1976, 46 (ill.), 49, 50; Schumacher c. 1850, 156r, 156v, 158r; Valdenaire 1919 (2d ed., 1926, 177).

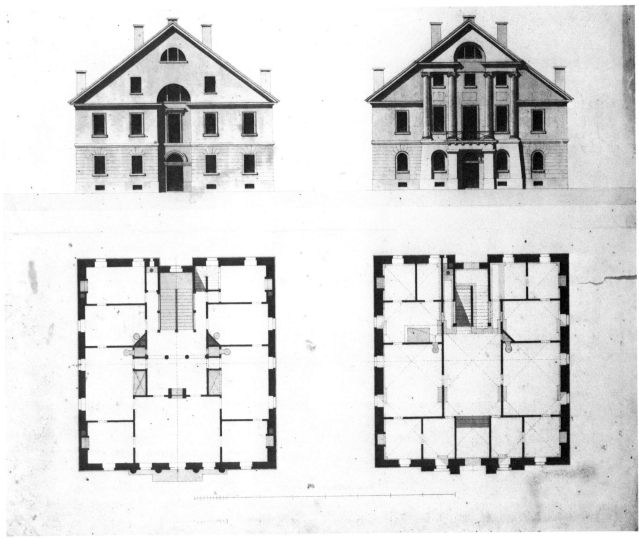

23

23, 24 (88.1, 88.2)
COUNTRY HOUSE, AARAU
Friedrich Weinbrenner, architect

In this project prepared for Switzerland, Weinbrenner combined vernacular elements with the more austere forms of neoclassicism. Its traditional, lofty profile, activated by two ranks of chimneys, evokes the protective roofs of Black Forest homes, and this imagery is reassuringly domestic.

Beneath the roof, however, stands an almost perfectly square structure of crystalline classical clarity. For the main elevation (cat. 23, top right) Weinbrenner hoisted an Ionic temple portico atop a rusticated basement. In both front and rear, the pediment is broken by a semicircular window, an element he often used. The interiors of this great house are selectively enriched; the grandest room is the *piano nobile* stairhall, screened by a pair of Ionic columns.

Weinbrenner had passed through Aarau when moving from Zürich to

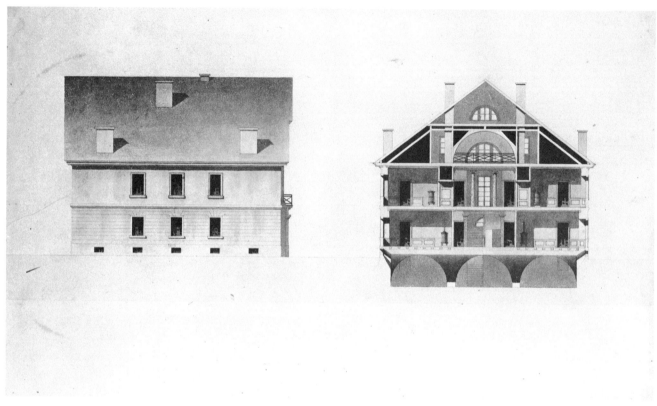

24

Lausanne in the late 1780s, and he visited Switzerland again briefly in 1792 and 1797. This project was probably commissioned by an acquaintance made on one of those visits. *D. B.*

BIBLIOGRAPHY

Sammlung 1847–58, 9; Schumacher c. 1850, 18r–19r.

25–27 (92.3, 92.1, 92.2)
HALF-TIMBERED COUNTRY
HOUSE
Ferdinand (?) Thierry, architect

This spectacular project for a country estate exemplifies the fascination with alpine architecture that flourished throughout Europe in the second quarter of the nineteenth century. While Weinbrenner had reserved half-timbering for farm buildings and modest houses, a member of the Thierry family, who signed two of these drawings (cats. 26, 27), here adapted it to the needs of the landed aristocracy. He created timber patterns that were significantly more intricate than those used in utilitarian structures (see cats. 28, 30, 31), although he eschewed the fancifulness of real *Fachwerk*, and he sheltered the house beneath broad eaves and behind sweeping verandas.

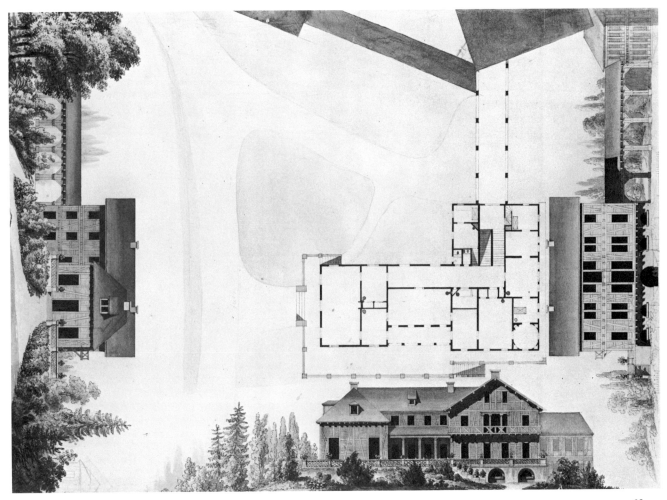

25

His new architectural vocabulary captured both the pretended simplicity and the essential pretentiousness of the nouveaux riches.

Thierry loved scenographic effects, and he maximized them in these rendered elevations. The compositions are made to appear unremittingly irregular, even though they are assembled from symmetrical parts—like the east and west blocks of the house and the north stable (cat. 26, foreground).

The latter is really a Palladian building translated into the rustic vernacular, and other features, like the sober colonnade of the north porch, help to invest the design with a measure of classical order. Still, these parts are attached to each other with studied dynamism; large elements are echoed by smaller ones, the south barns strike out obliquely (cat. 26), and the whole complex straggles over an irregular site.

The labeling of "Tab. III" (cat. 26) and "Tab. IV" (cat. 27) suggests that Thierry intended to publish them. They probably date from the first decade after Weinbrenner's death in 1826. *D. B.*

BIBLIOGRAPHY

Lankheit 1976, 47 and 48 (ill.), 49, 50.

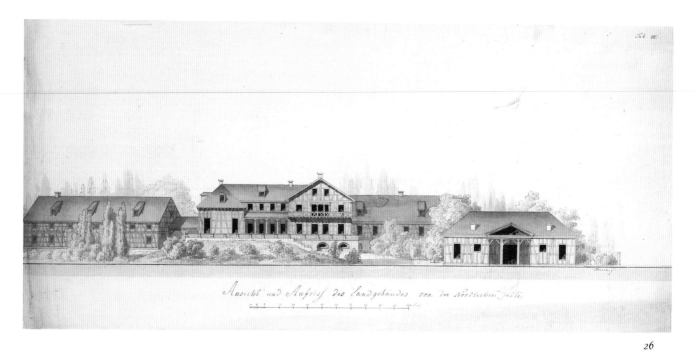

Ansicht und Aufriß des Landgebaudes von der nördlichen Seite

26

Ansicht und Aufriß des Landgebaudes von der östlichen Seite

27

28 (116.1)

FARMHOUSE, GROFISCH
School of Weinbrenner (Wilhelm
Thierry?)

This half-timbered farmhouse accommodated both humans and animals.
The residential portion of the ground
floor plan included a large room
("Stube") for the farmer as well as a
kitchen and sleeping chamber. The re-
mainder of the floor was devoted to
cattle stalls with feeding stations. A
combination of living and barn space
also occupied the upper floor, where
rooms for the farmer, farmhand, and
maid adjoined a storage room for
chaff.

   The elevation mixed half-timbering
with rusticated masonry. A double
stairway added unexpected formality
to the otherwise humble farmhouse
and indicated the rising status of farm-
ers in this age of agricultural reform; a
good tenant, well versed in the latest
methods, was highly valued by landowners. The inscription suggests that
Grofisch was located in "S[achsen]
Meiningen," in the Thuringian Forest.
Wilhelm Thierry, Ferdinand's brother,
was the court painter at Meiningen
from 1794 to 1810, before turning to
architecture and studying with Weinbrenner, and this may be his work.
Not far away was Gotha, where
Weinbrenner received several commissions (see cat. 51, checklist 28.1).

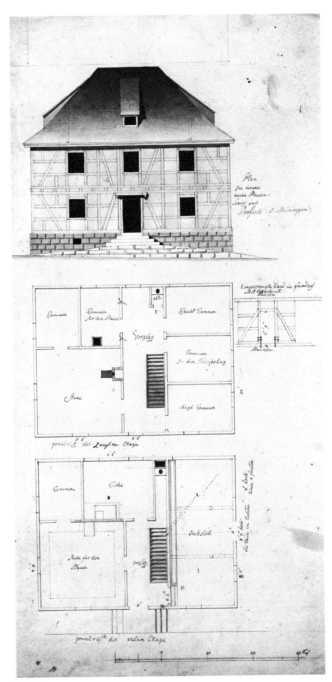

28

29 (126.1)
BARN *B*
School of Weinbrenner

This multipurpose masonry barn fits compactly under a snug hip roof. Simple geometric shapes, such as the unadorned central door, echo the forms of high-style neoclassicism.

The plan is divided into three bays. The left, marked "Sheuer" (barn), is used for storing hay and feed and for threshing. A cattle feeding station with its trough occupies the center of the building, while the right bay is divided into three parts, the largest of which is devoted to the cutting and storing of wood. Pigs, which were probably meant to enter the building through the semicircular opening in the rear, were sheltered in the middle-sized room, equipped with a second trough. The smallest space was reserved for geese, which could come and go through their own door at the upper right. *H. P.*

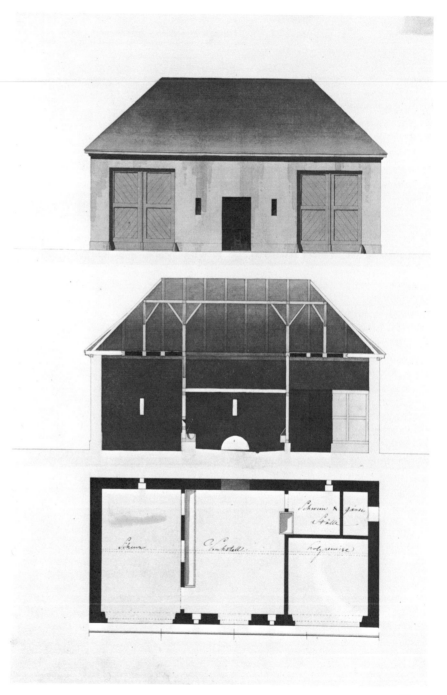

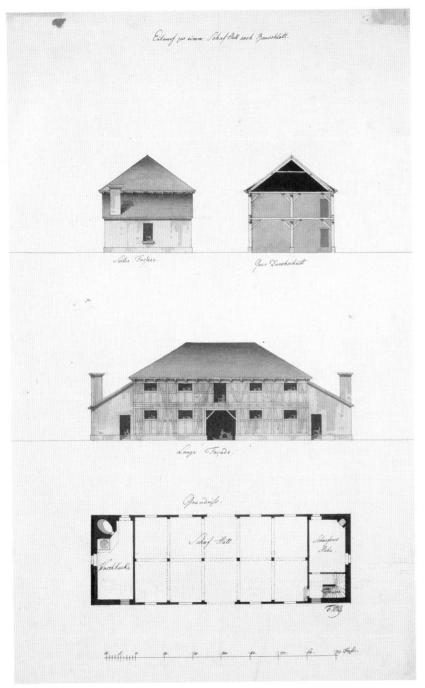

30 (120.1)
SHEEP SHED, BAUSCHLOTT
Friedrich Weinbrenner, architect

The village of Bauschlott, lying in a narrow valley some twenty kilometers east of Karlsruhe, was the site of a hunting lodge used by Grand Duke Karl Friedrich. He planned a new residence there in 1795, but work was actually carried out between 1805 and 1809, when Weinbrenner built a squire's house, modernized the existing barns, and added a Gothic dairy. These buildings still stand, gathered around the roughly rectangular farmyards and enclosed garden. The sheep shed, however, which was not part of the complex and stood elsewhere on the grounds, seems not to have survived.

Bauschlott's sheep were housed in the simple, half-timbered central block, where they could enjoy fresh air circulated through windows located high enough above their heads to prevent drafts. Two rooms of masonry construction flanked the barn. The left bay housed a washroom furnished with a basin and a stove, while the shepherd found simple quarters close to his flock at the other end of the building.

BIBLIOGRAPHY

Valdenaire 1919 (2d ed., 1926, 167–68).

31 (122.1)
HALF-TIMBERED BARN
School of Weinbrenner

This dignified but simple cattle barn should be compared with its Palladianized cousin (cat. 26, right foreground). In Weinbrenner's circle both the folk architecture of the German homeland and the heritage of the Italian Renaissance could be made subject to the same neoclassical canons. Indeed, it is sometimes difficult to see any distinction between classical modularity and the patterns of half-timbering.

Cattle stalls fill the right bay of the barn, with a big-portaled workroom (center) accessible to wagons. The rear wall, backing into the hillside, is shown as masonry construction. *D. B.*

31

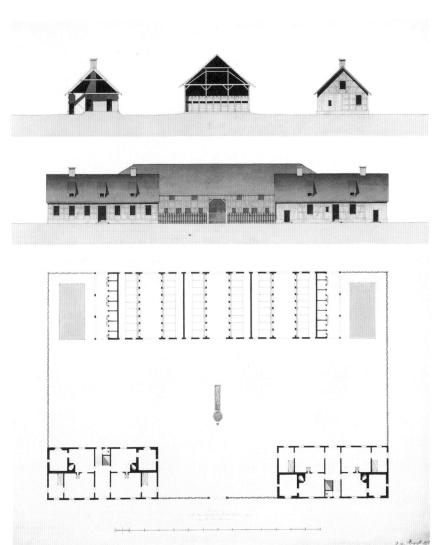

32

32 (112.1)
FARM, RITTERHECK
Friedrich Weinbrenner, architect

This drawing of August 1813 shows the tenant farm of Ritterheck, which Weinbrenner built on an island created by the Rhine's wandering course just seven kilometers northwest of Karlsruhe. Not far away stood the ancient village of Knielingen, whose wealth derived from that region's agriculture and horse breeding. It was this prosperity that interested David Seligmann, the Karlsruhe merchant and banker who had purchased Ritterheck in 1804.

Seligmann's farm was arranged by Weinbrenner according to the rectangular plan often used around 1800 for such model establishments. The rationalization of the rural economy was the key to making farms profitable. Two identical (but differently oriented) double cottages for laborers, built of a combination of masonry and half-timbering, flanked the entrance at the head of the orderly compound. A huge half-timbered cattle barn ran almost the entire length of the opposite side and protected the smaller buildings from wind. In the rectangular plots at each end of the barn, farm workers collected manure, the careful use of which was essential for increased agricultural productivity. Ritterheck was destroyed when the course of the Rhine was redefined by embankments in the 1820s. What remains of it now lies on the west bank of the river. *D. B.*

BIBLIOGRAPHY

Kolb 1813–16, vol. 3, 107; *Residenzstadt* 1858, 280–81; *Sammlung* 1847–58, 56; Valdenaire 1919 (2d ed., 1926, 169–70).

33

33, 34 (110.2, 110.1)
FARM, KATHARINENTAL
Friedrich Weinbrenner, architect

Katharinental, near Bauschlott in the rolling farmland east of Karlsruhe, was a tenant farm like Ritterheck, planned according to the most advanced agricultural theories (see fig. 4). The farm community was founded in the mid-eighteenth century, and Weinbrenner acted as its architect in 1808 and 1809, when these buildings were erected. During this period Katharinental claimed thirty inhabitants.

The general plan of the farm was as important as the designs for the individual buildings. The arrangement of the farm in a rectangle around a yard allowed for the greatest centralization and convenience, with the manager's house located at one end to give him a clear view of all activity. Moreover, the rectangular plan was ideal for col-

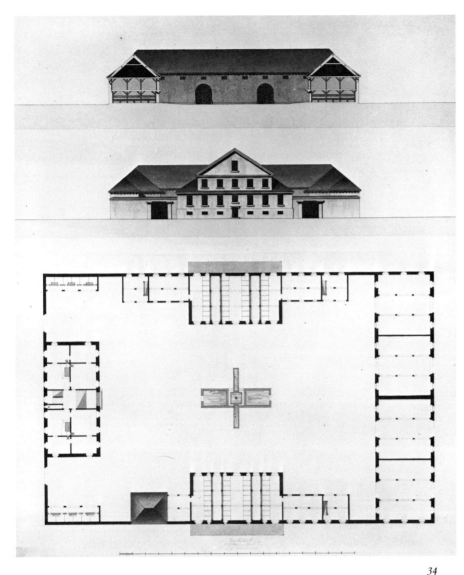

34

lecting the all-important manure that was plowed into the fields.

Pigs were sheltered in the small buildings close to the house, for they were partly sustained on household garbage and were the responsibility of the farmer's wife. On either side of the farmyard stood two large cattle barns, with sheds at their ends for sheep and wagons. A huge, wind-breaking hay barn loomed at the far end of the complex.

The main house at Katharinental exemplified Weinbrenner's most severe neoclassical version of Palladianism. Its masonry contrasted sharply with the half-timbered wings of the cow barns. The farm survives, although the house has been altered.

BIBLIOGRAPHY

Geier n.d.; *Sammlung* 1847–58, 55; Valdenaire 1919 (2d ed., 1926, 168–69).

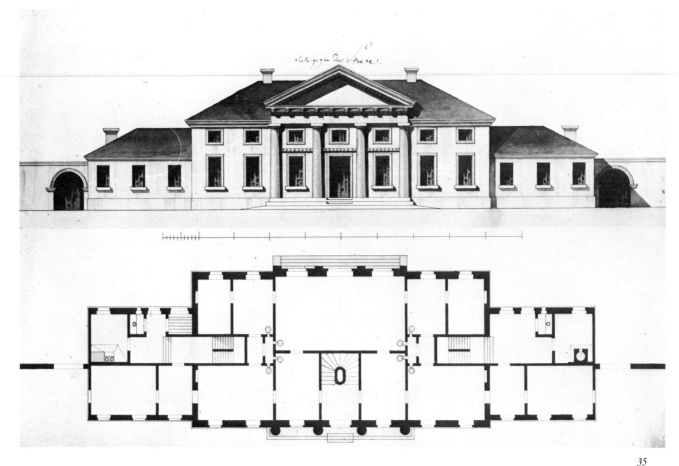

35

35, 36 (44.1, 44.2)
WEINBRENNER HOUSE,
KARLSRUHE
Friedrich Weinbrenner, architect

Shortly after his appointment as *Baudirektor* in 1801, Weinbrenner built a house for himself on a site located just inside the Ettlingen Gate, on the Schloss Strasse. Suggesting a vestigial square, Weinbrenner's house, like the stables for the margraves' palace opposite (see cat. 11), was placed some ten meters behind the street line. The design was forged from both well-established Anglo-Palladian elements and what Weinbrenner called Paestum-style forms. Its pedimented portico thus received squat Doric columns, a formula Weinbrenner reiterated in the adjacent Ettlingen Gate (1803).

The cubic clarity of this urban villa was articulated simply. On the street facade, four attached columns defined the central three bays, which were also linked by a string course with Vitruvian scroll ornament. The columns became pilasters on the garden elevation, and the ground floor openings were made round-headed.

From its inception, part of the building was used by Weinbrenner's own architectural school, which was started in 1800. This may explain certain idiosyncracies of the plan. Two distinct service areas, for example, were provided in the wings, and both were connected by staircases to the upper floor. Behind the main staircase

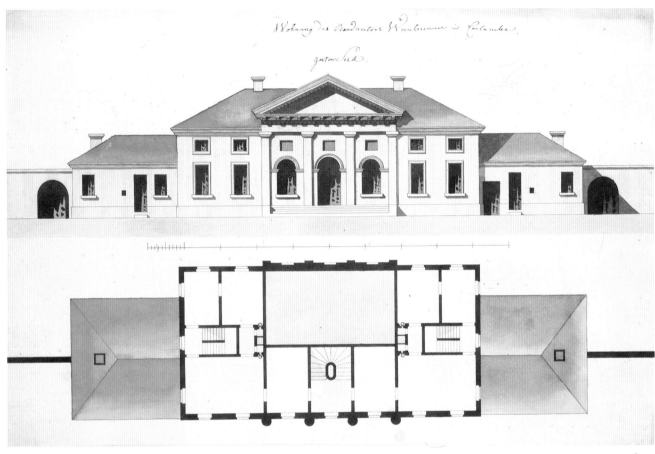

36

was a large, double-height room with
blind upper windows. Too dark for a
studio, this was surely used as a dining room or a reception area. The
house was demolished in 1873. *M. C.*

BIBLIOGRAPHY

Koebel [1920], 10; Schumacher c.
1850, 26r–27r; Staatliche Kunsthalle
1977, 65; Valdenaire 1919 (2d ed.,
1926, 95).

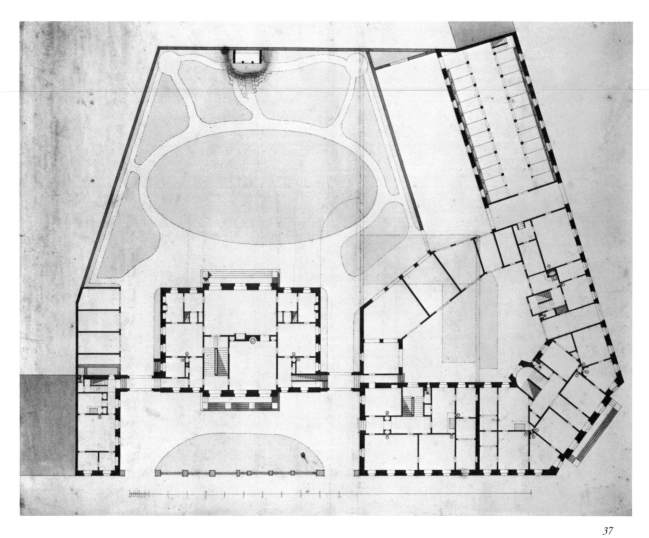

37

37 (48.1)
NORTHEAST RONDELLPLATZ
(BECK, JÖSLIN, AND
REUTLINGER HOUSES),
KARLSRUHE
Friedrich Weinbrenner, architect

In 1809 Margrave Friedrich, son of the
ruling Grand Duke Karl Friedrich, acquired three houses on the northeast
Rondellplatz and commissioned Weinbrenner to combine them into one
great residence (see fig. 5). The houses
involved were Weinbrenner's own Palladian villa for General von Beck
(1805), together with two houses by
C. T. Fischer, the Dr. Jöslin house
(1805), and the Elkan Reutlinger or
"Rondell" house (1809–10). The Beck
house was situated on the Schloss
Strasse to the north of the Rondellplatz (left) and adjoined the Jöslin
house, which was attached in turn to
the Reutlinger house facing the Rondellplatz (right).

   Weinbrenner's important alterations
of 1809 and 1810 are shown in this
ground plan together with the dotted
ghosts of former structures. A new
stable building was placed to the south
of the extended and relandscaped
Beck garden (top right), and the old
outbuildings were cleared to build

a court serving both the Jöslin and Reutlinger houses. The small temple (top left) remained from the original scheme. A covered passageway linked the Beck and Jöslin houses, while the Jöslin and Reutlinger houses were connected by doors pierced through the party wall on the upper floor (not visible in cat. 37). In 1830 the complex was again divided. Freifrau von Gesau bought the Reutlinger house and the Lesegesellschaft (Library Society) acquired the Beck house (see checklist 50.1). All the buildings were demolished after severe damage in the Second World War. *M. C.*

BIBLIOGRAPHY

Geier n.d.; Valdenaire 1919 (2d ed., 1926, 96–98).

38 (82.1)
PAINTER'S HOUSE,
KARLSRUHE (?)
Friedrich Weinbrenner, architect

This project appears in both Heinrich Geier's sketchbook and in the *Sammlung von Grundplänen*, where it is described as the house of a painter. It is unlikely that it was built, but the archaic Greek ruggedness of its Doric columns suggests that the project should be placed in the period between the early designs for the Rathaus (c. 1794) and those for Weinbrenner's own house (1801). It may have been intended for the painter Asmus Jacob Carstens, with whom Weinbrenner had traveled to Rome in 1792.

The front elevation shows a Doric portico carrying a balcony over the entrance; the roof line above is a cramped juxtaposition of pediments and gable ends, fundamentally Palladian in form. Continuity with the outbuildings is achieved by the uninterrupted rustication of the ground story. The planning facilitated two quite distinct purposes for the building, with the front of the complex devoted to the domestic uses of a middle-class residence. The rear, however, forming the other three sides of the atrium-like courtyard, had much larger rooms on its upper floor that

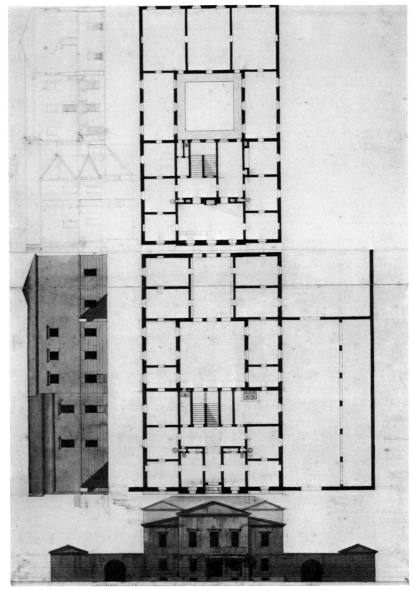

38

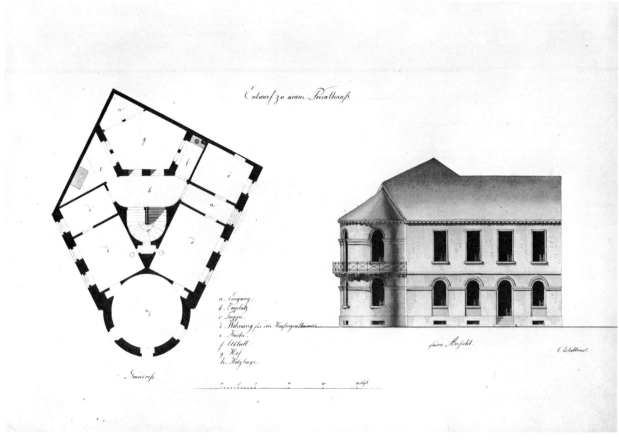

Entwurf zu einem Privathauß.

a. *Eingang.*
b. *Vorplatz.*
c. *Treppe.*
d. *Wohnung für den Hauseigenthümer.*
e. *Küche.*
f. *Abtritt.*
g. *Hof.*
h. *Holzlage.*

Grundriß.

innere Ansicht. *Gesichtsbau.*

39

were adapted to the requirements of the painter's work. The side rooms, with their high windows, were used as galleries, while the corner rooms at the rear, lit from one side only, were the painter's studios. Two large courtyards to either side of the building would have provided stabling. *M. C.*

BIBLIOGRAPHY

Geier n.d.; *Sammlung* 1847–58, 17; Valdenaire 1919 (2d ed., 1926, 138).

39 (74.1)
CORNER HOUSE, KARLSRUHE
Friedrich Arnold, architect (?)

This unidentified corner house was drawn by C. Eichelkraut, who worked as a draftsman for Friedrich Arnold, one of Weinbrenner's most successful students. Karlsruhe's circular plan created many difficult, acute-angled corner sites, and this design embodied one of the solutions frequently employed by Weinbrenner's followers: The staircase was placed in the center and a circular turret filled the angle.

The remaining rooms were arrayed along the two street facades. A heavy course at the springing level of the round arches on the ground floor was continued above them as window hoods, suggesting an encircling arcade at street level and uniting the disparate geometrical solids out of which the house was composed. *M. C.*

BIBLIOGRAPHY

Architectural Association 1982, 26 (ill.); assistance from Gerhard Everke; Staatliche Kunsthalle 1977, 112 (ill.), 117.

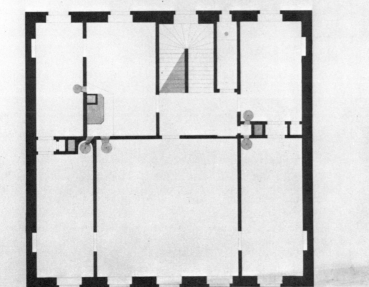

40 (78.1)
ATTACHED HOUSE, KARLSRUHE (?)
School of Weinbrenner

This unidentified design exhibits the canonical features of the town houses with which Weinbrenner filled the city south of the Lange Strasse in the second decade of the century. The ground floor was rusticated in the Palladian manner, and a round-arched opening led to the courtyard behind; such passages were necessitated every forty feet by the Karlsruhe fire regulations. The rest of the facade was rendered in smooth stucco relieved by several plastic elements: window hoods supported on consoles, a balcony with massier curved consoles, and a modillion eaves-cornice. The hoods and consoles were painted in a different color from the stucco to emphasize their three-dimensionality.

The height of the complete facade was controlled according to the building regulations of 1804, which had probably been drafted by Weinbrenner. This code established house heights according to the width of the street and the proximity of the site to the town center. The plans of such houses were normally simple, provided the site was straightforward. Here the staircase was placed at the rear with the major rooms aligned along the front of the building. *M. C.*

BIBLIOGRAPHY

Ehrenberg 1908, 74ff; Huber 1954, 70ff.

41

41–43 (56.2, 56.3, 56.1)
HOLB HOUSE, KARLSRUHE
Friedrich Weinbrenner, architect

The Zähringerstrasse was rapidly developing for middle-class housing in the second decade of the century, despite the awkwardness of some sites bordering the *Landgrabe* (canal) to its south. This house, built for building contractor Christoph Holb in 1815, was located on one of those crooked sites west of the Marktplatz. In the first, larger version (cats. 41, 42), Weinbrenner sought to distinguish the house from its rowhouse neighbors by the use of a pediment, a solution already employed in the house for the apothecary Sommerschuh (1814), at the other end of the Zähringerstrasse. The individuality of the building was

42

further emphasized by the recession of the central three bays beneath a huge blind arch that broke into the pediment. The pediment, in turn, was filled in Palladian fashion by a thermal window—the oft-used Weinbrenner motif.

The executed building (cat. 43) was a less individualistic (and cheaper) two-story structure, preserving, however, the sophisticated planning solution devised for the first design. An apse-ended courtyard, entrance to which was admitted by a wide passage through the center of the house, was used as a fulcrum for turning the two axes of the site. The difficult corners to either side of the curved end of the courtyard were snugly fitted with a circular room and a round-ended staircase, freeing the rest of the house for a normative alignment of rooms on two axes. On the upper floor the spatial sequence was completed by a hexagonal hall facing the courtyard. *M. C.*

BIBLIOGRAPHY

Sammlung 1847–58, 3; Staatliche Kunsthalle 1977, 116–17, 123–25 (ill.); Valdenaire 1919 (2d ed., 1926, 135).

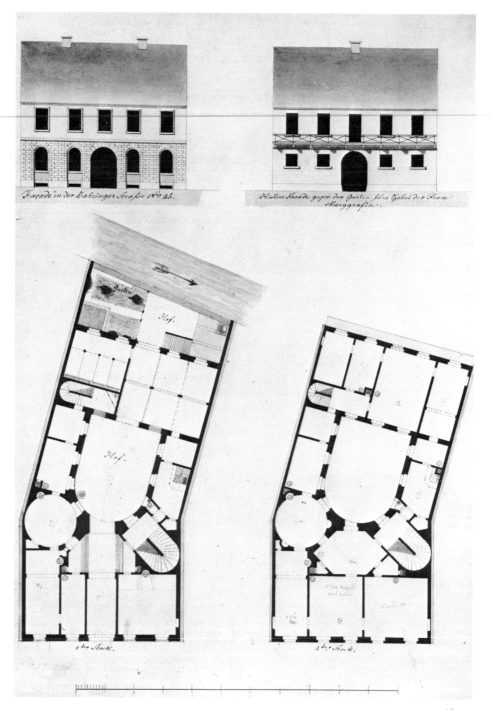

Façade in der Zähringer Strasse No 45.

Hintere Façade gegen den Garten: Ihro Hoheit der Frau Marggräfin.

Garten

Hof.

Hof.

1 ter Stock.

2 ter Stock.

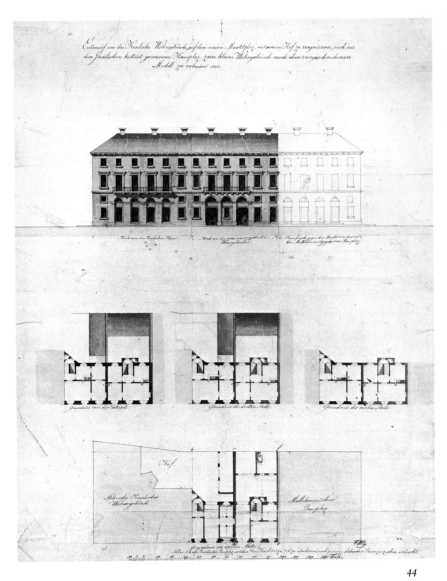

44

built a house for him in 1804 that established the model for the additions made in 1812 when Kusel acquired the neighboring sites, and also for the houses on the opposite side of the square. This drawing shows the original Kusel house (top left) together with the designs for the 1812 addition (top center and plans) and the proposal (in outline) for another house attached to the north. The entire block was deemed significant enough to feature as a detail in the 1822 city map published by Weinbrenner.

While the elements of the Kusel houses were typical of Weinbrenner's many attached houses in Karlsruhe (see cat. 40), the rhythmic play of parts—making the several houses into one composition—was unusual. In the drawing the addition of 1812 is separated from the existing building by a dotted line. Six new bays were added, including three wide roundheaded bays placed asymmetrically within the addition but central to the projected block as a whole. The real internal divisions of the houses were thus disguised. The plans show that the leftmost arched openings provided access to the extended courtyard of the original Kusel house, while the third one opened onto an independent courtyard. The rooms in the front of the building were used as shops. *M. C.*

44 (52.1)
KUSEL HOUSES, KARLSRUHE
Friedrich Weinbrenner, architect

The court agent Jacob Kusel was a typical representative of the entrepreneurial class in Karlsruhe. He was a partner in a banking house and, with the brothers Model, he opened the city's first drapery business in 1815. In 1802 Kusel had acquired a prime site on the corner of the Zähringerstrasse and the Marktplatz, to the north of the Rathaus site. Here Weinbrenner

BIBLIOGRAPHY

Fecht 1887–88, 419; Goldschmit 1915, 55, 425; Lankheit 1976, 10, 11–12 (ill.); *Sammlung* 1847–58, 5; Staatliche Kunsthalle 1977, 114, 121 (ill.); Valdenaire 1919 (2d ed., 1926, 96); Valdenaire 1948, 441, 443–44.

45, 46 (62.1, 62.2)
HERTZER HOUSE, BADEN-BADEN
Friedrich Weinbrenner, architect

Weinbrenner's work in Baden-Baden was extensive, although many of his plans were unrealized. These drawings, one dated 1824, show an unbuilt house for Captain Hertzer, probably intended for a site where the Lange Strasse enters the Hindenburgplatz. In its superposition of entrance, pilasters, and pediment on a narrow corner facade, the design was similar to the house Weinbrenner built at the corner of the Lange Strasse and the Waldhornstrasse in Karlsruhe in 1810, but in other respects it was very different from houses in the capital. The roof was emphatically pitched and crested with a clock tower, perhaps in response to similar features in the still medieval townscape of the spa city, while in contrast a giant pilaster order established a vocabulary that distinguished the building from its immediate neighbors.

The planning of the building represents another solution to the problem of the acute-angled corner site. The entrance, framed by baseless Doric columns, opened onto a wide passage driven through the heart of the house to the court at the rear. Around this passage were arrayed a sequence of curved and polygonal shapes, and above it rose a great, square-bayed stairhall with divided staircase. On the *piano nobile* a circular *Kabinett* with a dome filled the corner angle, with an oval double-height room behind it and the other rooms in enfilade along the two sides of the building. The sequence of geometrical shapes

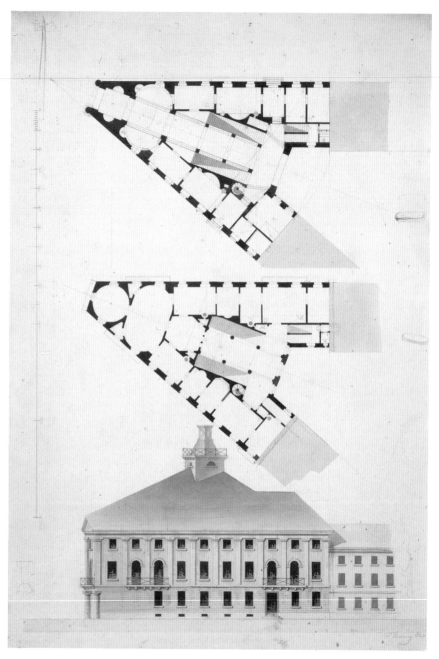

45

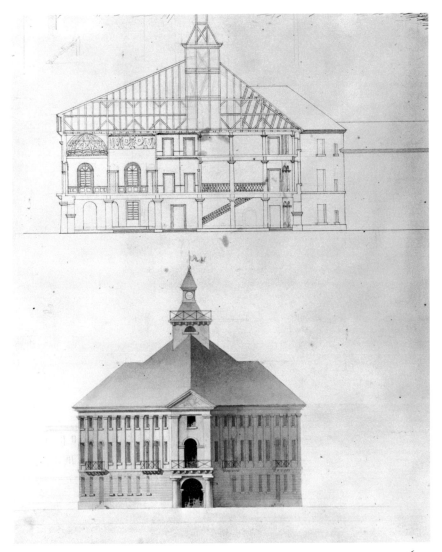

may have been suggested by Parisian prototypes. *M. C.*

BIBLIOGRAPHY

Lankheit 1976, 7 (ill.), 8, 9 (ill.), 10; *Sammlung* 1847–58, 21; Schumacher c. 1850, 36r–38r; Staatliche Kunsthalle 1977, 117–18, 126–27 (ill.); Valdenaire 1919 (2d ed., 1926, 138).

46

47

47, 48 (152.2, 152.1)
ARSENAL, KARLSRUHE
Friedrich Weinbrenner, architect

Conceived in the spirit of the great building projects of Roman antiquity, Weinbrenner's design for an arsenal clearly belongs with his student work of the 1790s. The interior courtyard (cat. 47) lies within the central block. It is evidently a copy of Staatliche Kunsthalle P.K.I 483-9, which is dated 1795. The drawing exploits perspective to theatrical effect, although, unlike many similar studies, it was not adapted for publication in Weinbrenner's *Architektonisches Lehrbuch*. One views the courtyard through a pair of archaic, unfluted Doric columns, recalling those Weinbrenner had sketched at Paestum.

At the center of the courtyard (and of the converging perspective lines), Weinbrenner has shown a statue of Minerva, the Roman goddess of war, seated and dressed in battle attire. This was probably modeled on the ancient statue of that goddess that he would have seen in the Capitoline courtyard in Rome. The cannonballs stacked on either side of the sculpture indicate the building's function.

A section through the outer courtyard (cat. 48) may be in Weinbrenner's hand. It is rendered in the severe, linear style promoted by the painter

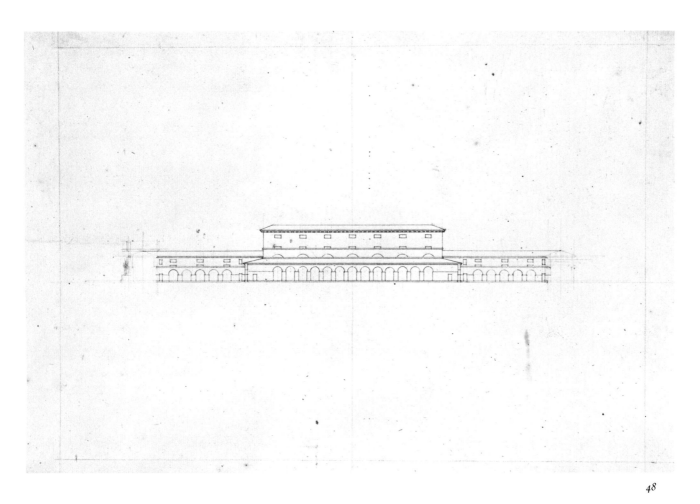

48

Asmus Jacob Carstens, whom he had accompanied to Italy in 1792, and the great horizontal sweep of the exterior is reminiscent of Weinbrenner's 1794 project for the Karlsruhe Rathaus. The central block is flanked by two-story wings that turn outward to encircle the viewer.

While a student in Berlin in 1792 Weinbrenner had been particularly impressed by the great horizontal mass of Andreas Schlüter's baroque arsenal built in 1698 and 1699. The young architect may have sought to surpass Schlüter with his own project, using a new vocabulary in which the scale of Roman imperial architecture was freely combined with Greek details. *R. W.*

BIBLIOGRAPHY

Architectural Association 1982, 34; Robert Rosenblum, *Transformations in Late Eighteenth Century Art* (Princeton: Princeton University Press, 1967), 147; Schirmer et al. 1975, 18; Sinos 1981, 26; Staatliche Kunsthalle 1978, 49, 53; Valdenaire 1919 (2d ed., 1926, 41, 46); Weinbrenner 1958, 47.

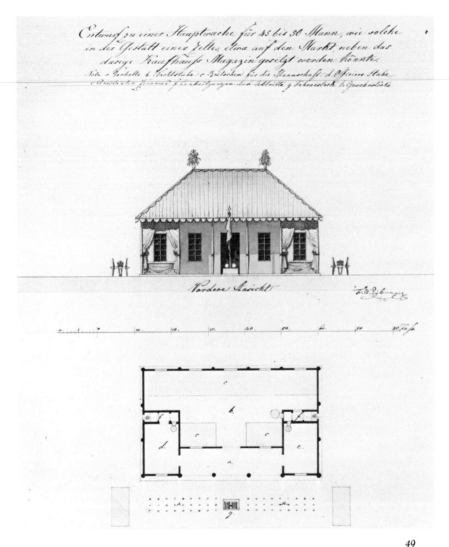

Two palm-frond finials mark where the posts of an actual tent would poke through the canvas. Flanking the structure are two cannons. The plan provides accommodation for soldiers and officers as well as an area for the storage of ceremonial carriages. According to the somewhat ambiguous inscription, the guard house was to be placed in the Marktplatz near a warehouse.

Although the drawing is not dated, the guard house was probably erected for the visit of Empress Josephine on November 28, 1805. In honor of her three-day sojourn, the city's major thoroughfares were decorated by Weinbrenner in a festive manner, including the erection of a one-hundred-foot column surmounted by a glittering sphere. It is likely that the guard house was left standing for the visit of Napoleon the following January, and for the festivities surrounding the wedding in Paris of Stephanie de Beauharnais, the emperor's adopted daughter, and Karl, the crown prince of Baden, in April 1806. *R. W.*

BIBLIOGRAPHY

Goldschmit 1915, 29–30; Lankheit 1976, 41 (ill.), 49, 50.

49

49 (160.1)
GUARD HOUSE, KARLSRUHE
Friedrich Weinbrenner, architect

Signed by Weinbrenner, this drawing shows a guard house planned to serve up to fifty men. Its brightly colored and draperied form directly recalls the work of Charles Percier and Pierre Fontaine, the official architects of Napoleon and the particular favorites of the Empress Josephine. The guard house was a temporary structure conceived in the spirit of a tent, like one of the interiors created by Percier and Fontaine at Malmaison (1800), with a gaily striped pink and blue roof, scalloped cornice, and curtained end bays.

50

50 (166.1)
SYNAGOGUE, KARLSRUHE
Friedrich Weinbrenner, architect

Within the relatively liberal political climate of Baden, the Jewish community in Karlsruhe had thrived in the late eighteenth century, even though religious toleration was not officially granted by the state until 1808. By 1791 their synagogue at the corner of the Kronenstrasse and Lange (now Kaiser-) Strasse had become too small,

and in May 1798 the congregation asked the young Weinbrenner to design a new structure. Construction began on June 10, and the first services were held in the sanctuary in 1800. The main facade was completed in 1806, and the rabbi's house, to its right, could be occupied in 1810.

The design was an evocative amalgam of the diverse historical sources that were newly available in the late eighteenth century. The entrance portal and the arcade above it were

Gothic, paying homage to the medieval architecture that Weinbrenner had begun to admire during the year spent as a student in Vienna. It was also in Vienna, in the fall of 1791, that the music-loving architect had attended two of the first performances of Mozart's *Zauberflöte*, one of which was conducted by the composer himself. The opera's Egyptian setting may have inspired the other striking feature of the facade—the twin, three-story gate pylons that alluded to the ancient and eastern character of Judaism. Weinbrenner could have studied these details in the 1779 German translation of Frederik Norden's *Voyage d'Egypte et de Nubie* (Copenhagen, 1755). Such sources precipitated the arrival of this Egyptian fashion in Germany nearly two decades before the Napoleonic exploration of the Nile (the findings of which were published between 1809 and 1828) began to spread the taste elsewhere. Indeed, Weinbrenner's synagogue was the first large Egyptian building to be erected since antiquity: the first building of the Egyptian Revival.

Two baseless Doric columns in the building's atrium-like courtyard are barely visible through the portal, and they are evidence of yet a third component of Weinbrenner's education— the late-eighteenth-century rediscovery of ancient Greek architecture. Weinbrenner's visits to Paestum in 1794 and 1796 made him one of the first German architects to have seen such columns firsthand. Beyond the colonnaded courtyard lay the pedimented sanctuary, which contained classrooms beneath the women's galleries. The synagogue was destroyed by fire in 1871 and its successor was demolished by the Kristallnacht mobs. *D. B.*

BIBLIOGRAPHY

Architectural Association 1982, 20, 37; Geier n.d.; Hammer-Schenk 1981, vol. 1, 58, 63, 235–40; Lankheit 1976, 6 (ill.), 8, 39; *Sammlung* 1847–58, 28; Schumacher c. 1850, 64r–66r; Sinos 1981, 26–29, 28 (ill.); Staatliche Kunsthalle 1977, 57–58, 66–67, 66 (ill.); Valdenaire 1919 (2d ed., 1926, 65–66).

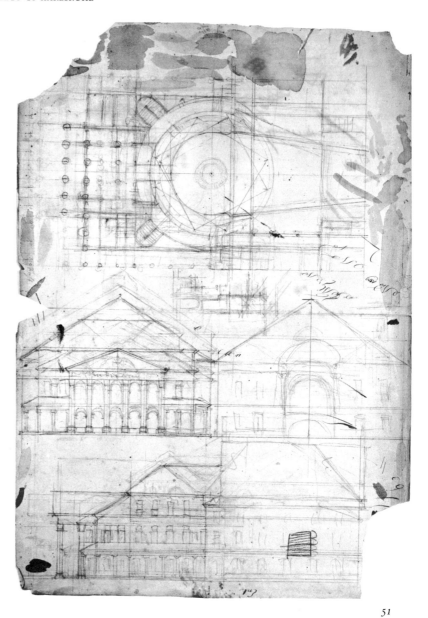

51

51 (164.1)
THEATER, GOTHA
Friedrich Weinbrenner, architect

As a student in Rome, Weinbrenner had designed a theater based on antique prototypes, the first of a lifelong series of innovative projects experimenting with this building type. His later work included new theaters in Baden-Baden and Leipzig as well as his native city. This drawing is for a theater project in Gotha, in Thuringia, almost 200 miles northwest of Karlsruhe. It can be dated to 1812 and is probably in Weinbrenner's hand.

The front elevation of this theater (center left) is not unlike Weinbrenner's Karlsruhe Theater of 1807 and 1808, with a rather conservatively Palladian six-column portico and hipped roof. Rough lines indicate an alternate roof line. To the right of the front elevation, a second elevation shows the rear facade with a high gable, a formula adopted for the front facade of his Leipzig Theater in 1817.

The plan depicts a lobby filled with columns that carry the module of the portico inside. Beyond lies the great horseshoe-shaped auditorium, with a circular reflected ceiling plan at the center. There are a number of sketches on the verso, several of which seem to be for the staging of a marionette show.

Weinbrenner's design for the theater at Gotha was never built. In March 1817 the architect traveled to Leipzig, where his major theater project was nearing completion. He stopped in Gotha where he reported that he was "very honorably received by the Duke of Gotha," but the theater project languished. Karl Friedrich Schinkel also made an unsuccessful proposal at this time. Finally, between 1837 and 1840 a theater was built in Gotha to the design of Gustav Eberhard. *R. W.*

BIBLIOGRAPHY

Assistance of Claudia Elbert; Schumacher c. 1850, 108r–112r; Valdenaire 1919 (2d ed., 1926, 227).

52

52 (172.1)
CEMETERY GATE, KARLSRUHE
Friedrich Weinbrenner, architect (?)

One of the chief obstacles to the expansion of Karlsruhe in general and the construction of Weinbrenner's Marktplatz in particular was the city's main cemetery, which lay behind the old Protestant church on the main axis of the Schloss Strasse. The overtaxed graveyard was expanded in the 1770s, and between 1803 and 1804 an entirely new cemetery was opened south of

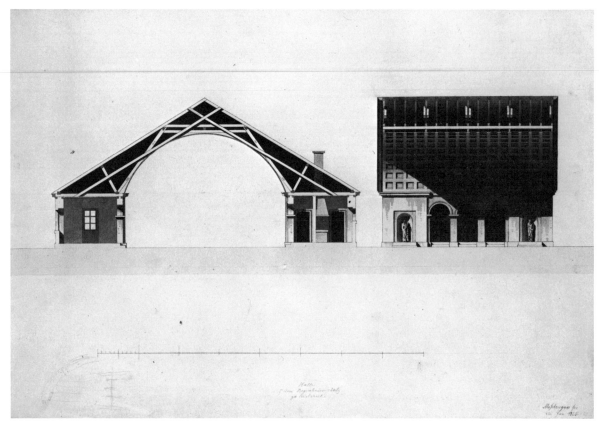

53

the Waldhornstrasse. This accomplished a great sanitary reform, and, for the same purpose, all burials within churches in Karlsruhe and Durlach were banned, as was the movement of corpses except at night and in cold weather.

This cemetery gate was probably designed in connection with the establishment of the Waldhornstrasse burial ground. A severe neoclassical structure, it resembled Weinbrenner's city-gate projects. One entered the cemetery through a screen of Doric columns and pilasters and beneath a blind arch with relief carving. Beyond the entrance rose a shallow barrel

vault. A small chapel occupied the room at left, balanced by an attendant's station at right.

The two sculptural groups indicated on the front and rear elevations represent a romantic revival of a medieval German iconographic tradition. On the outer tympanum, facing the city, was an image of Frau Welt, the seductive personification of the material world, who, according to a thirteenth-century poem, was ultimately vanquished by Christ. From the rear she is traditionally shown in a state of mortal decay; a scene of the Crucifixion was appropriately substituted. *R. W.*

53 (176.1)
CEMETERY HALL, KARLSRUHE
Friedrich Weinbrenner or August Mossbrugger, architect (?)

This project for a cemetery hall seems to have been based on the model of French funeral wagon depots. As shown in the longitudinal and transverse sections, the building was an open-ended structure with a wide, barrel-vaulted central space large enough for two hearses. To either side were narrow chambers; that at the right, heated by a stove, was presumably intended for the attendant. Above the barrel vault, an elaborate truss supported the roof.

Although greatly diminished in scale, this design is related to Weinbrenner's student project for a princely tomb, with its great barrel-vaulted central chamber lined with funerary monuments; that, in turn, recalled the work of Etienne-Louis Boullée. This drawing is inscribed in pencil "Halle/auf den Begrabnissplatz/zu Carlsruhe," and it was signed and dated in January 1825 by August Mossbrugger, Weinbrenner's former pupil and the drawing instructor in his architectural school. *R. W.*

54 (174.1)
MORTUARY, KARLSRUHE
Friedrich Weinbrenner, architect (?)

A city mortuary was proposed for Karlsruhe as early as 1790, but it was deemed too expensive by city officials. The idea was revived in 1812, and it was probably at this time that this modest proposal was submitted. The project, however, was still being debated well into the 1820s, and nothing was built until much later.

The mortuary was to be a severe building, T-shaped in plan, with little architectural detail. The wall surfaces were plainly rendered with no window moldings, and the pilasters lacked capitals. Despite its small scale, the interior was to be partitioned into several rooms, including a morgue, a separate chamber for murder victims, and a kitchen, living room, and sleeping quarters for the attendants. *R. W.*

BIBLIOGRAPHY

Fecht 1887–88, 552–53.

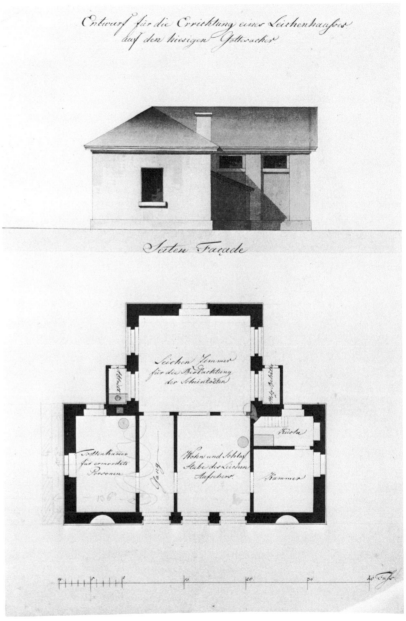

54

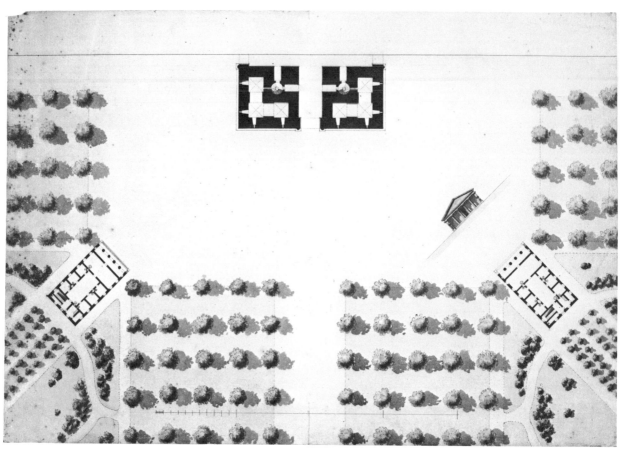

55

55 (180.1)
VICTORY MONUMENT, LEIPZIG
Friedrich Weinbrenner, architect

Although it is the Battle of Waterloo in 1815 that is celebrated today, it was Napoleon's decisive defeat at Leipzig in October 1813 (the so-called Battle of the Nations) that precipitated the collapse of the French empire. Baden had fought on the side of the French, but by November she had been compelled to ally herself with Napoleon's foes. This seems to have kindled Wein-

brenner's newly emerging German nationalist pride and prompted his commemoration of the Prussian victory with his *Ideen zu einem teutschen Nationaldenkmal*, published in 1814. "Inspired by the great deeds of the allied powers," he wrote in the text, "I undertake to portray in sculpture their glorious victory against the French emperor at Leipzig . . . in a national public monument dedicated to the well-being of Germany and the general good of Europe, and to keep its memory alive for posterity."

This drawing is a half-site plan for Weinbrenner's proposed monument at the battlefield. Unlike a group of drawings now in the Staatliche Kunsthalle, this one was not produced before the publication of his pamphlet, in which only a plan of the monument appeared. Indeed, Weinbrenner referred in the text to his inability to provide a site plan because of a lack of knowledge about the battlefield.

The monument was to be colossal. Each side of the base, shown in half plan, was to be 60 meters long, and around it Weinbrenner created a vast landscape approximately 300 meters in breadth. Evenly spaced rows of oak trees, symbolic of Germany, surrounded the monument and defined broad promenades. On the diagonal axes small Doric temples, one of which is shown in elevation, contained quarters for attending guards. The monument consisted of a 10-meter base, above which rose a Doric temple whose cella was to contain a pantheon of German monarchs and war heroes (see fig. 6). Its roof was a stepped pyramid surmounted by a group of allegorical sculpture portraying Love, Wisdom, and Strength crowned by Victory. The project was derived from Weinbrenner's student reconstruction of the Mausoleum of Halicarnassus made in the 1790s, and, ironically, it also recollected his proposals of 1802 and 1803 for monuments honoring the French republic and Napoleon.

In 1814 and 1815 an official competition for the Leipzig memorial was declared by Ludwig I of Bavaria, to whom Weinbrenner sent this proposal, but nothing was built. A victory monument on the Leipzig battlefield was not constructed until the turn of the twentieth century, when the commission was awarded to Bruno Schmitz. *R. W.*

BIBLIOGRAPHY

Architectural Association 1982, 42–43; Geier n.d.; Lankheit 1979, 25–31; Schumacher c. 1850, 207r; Staatliche Kunsthalle 1977, 79; Valdenaire 1919 (2d ed., 1926, 286–91); Weinbrenner 1814.

56 (194.15)
BELLE
ALLIANCE MEMORIAL
Friedrich Weinbrenner, architect

Weinbrenner, perhaps realizing that his Leipzig monument would not be built, also designed a war memorial for the Belle Alliance battlefield near Waterloo. Rendered here in perspective, the monument is set on a large base (containing a crypt) with urns at each corner. To each side stand equestrian statues of the Duke of Wellington and Marshall Blücher, the victorious allied leaders. The monument is capped by Victory crowning a personification of Europe.

Weinbrenner probably conceived of the design soon after the battle, in late 1815. He had finished the project by 1816 but could not find an interested publisher for his *Vorschlag zu einem Sieges-Denkmal für das Schlachtfeld bei Belle-Alliance* until 1818. In it he wrote: "We are indebted to the allied powers for the accomplishment of peace on the 18th of June 1815, which again blooms in Europe for the good fortune of its inhabitants. Thus, the battle of Belle Alliance, not far from Waterloo, also deserves to be honored by a monument on the battlefield. Through this victory, all fortunate people should be united from the Tagus to the Volga."

This drawing of the monument was probably executed after the publication of the project in 1818 and before the printing of the 1824 fascicles of his *Lehrbuch*, in which the project appeared as an exercise in perspective. In the latter year a Belle Alliance monument was erected on the battlefield to the design of another architect. *R. W.*

BIBLIOGRAPHY

Lankheit 1976, 25–27, 26 (ill.); Lankheit 1979, 31–35; Valdenaire 1919 (2d ed., 1926, 291–96); Weinbrenner 1818; Weinbrenner 1810–25, vol. 1, 77–80, pl. XL.

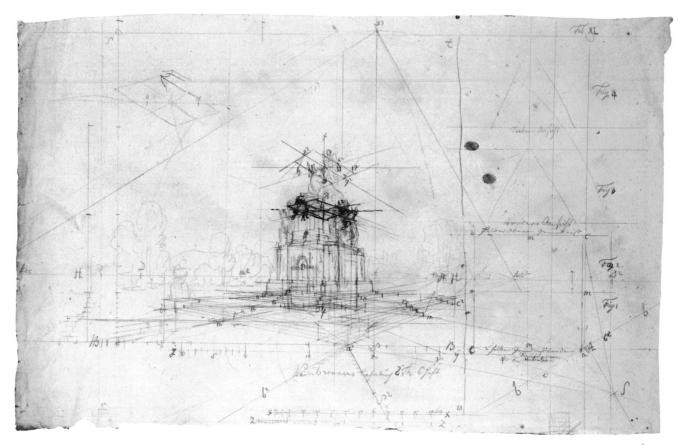

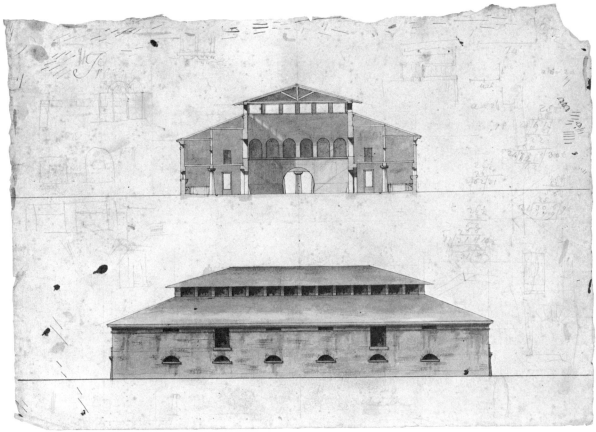

57

57, 58 (144.2, 144.1)
RIDING SCHOOL, KARLSRUHE
Friedrich Weinbrenner, architect

Riding schools had been founded as early as the sixteenth century in Italy and Spain, and by the eighteenth century many European cities had established their own academies for instruction in proper horsemanship. These two drawings are for Weinbrenner's project for a riding school in Karlsruhe. From the Italian watermark on the front elevation and ground plan (cat. 58) one can conclude that they were executed during Weinbrenner's stay in Rome during the 1790s. Indeed, a figure study on the verso showing the drinking contest between Herakles and Dionysus (cat. 58), seems to be the exercise of an architectural student, and sketches on the other verso (cat. 57) are related to either Weinbrenner's student project for the Karlsruhe Rathaus or his reconstruction of the Roman Baths of Hippias, both dating from the 1790s.

The riding school was designed as a basilica, with the side aisles transformed into stalls and the central exercise area illuminated by clerestory windows. The laconic elevations are relieved by a row of small thermal windows on the sides and an unfluted Doric portico across the front, reminiscent of the primitive Greek orders he had seen at Paestum. Weinbrenner may have chosen this style because of the advanced development of horsemanship in ancient Greece, epitomized in Xenophon's treatise "On Equitation."

An alternate sketch for the main facade can be seen at the upper left border of cat. 58, in which Weinbren-

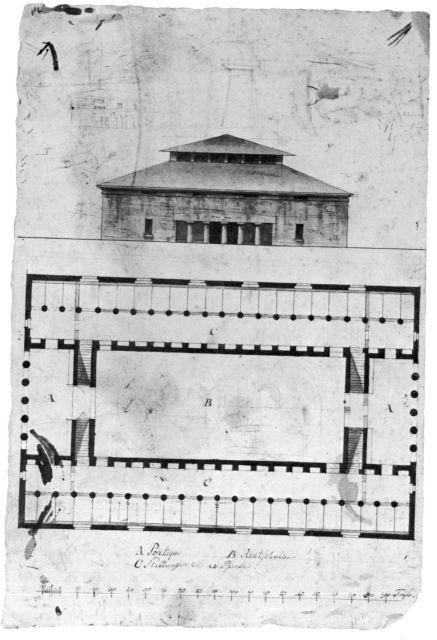

A Portique   B Reutschule
C Stallungen zu 12 Pferde

58

ner inserted a row of windows above the portico. This sketch prefigures a second design that Weinbrenner made for the riding school, which is not represented in the collection. In addition to the second-story windows, this revised project was distinguished by a great equestrian frieze that wrapped around the entire building.

The riding school was originally planned for a plot on the Rüpperer Strasse but was never built. Heinrich Hübsch designed a stud farm on this site between 1837 and 1839, perhaps as a gesture to his teacher's early project. *R. W.*

BIBLIOGRAPHY

Geier n.d.; Lankheit 1976, 42 (ill.), 49, 50; *Sammlung* 1847–58, 57; Schumacher c. 1850, 93r–95v; Sinos 1981, 24 (ill.); Valdenaire 1919 (2d ed., 1926, 257–58, 276).

59 (156.1)
TURKISH BATH, BADEN-BADEN (?)
Friedrich Weinbrenner, architect

Although bathing was not generally popular in Europe until the 1830s, taking the waters in Baden–Baden had long been practiced because of the imagined therapeutic effect of its natural springs. One of Weinbrenner's most delightful drawings, marked in another hand as being his work, is this design for a Turkish bath. Perhaps related to the baths he designed for the spa city, the drawing is labeled "Tab. VIII.," suggesting that Weinbrenner intended publication.

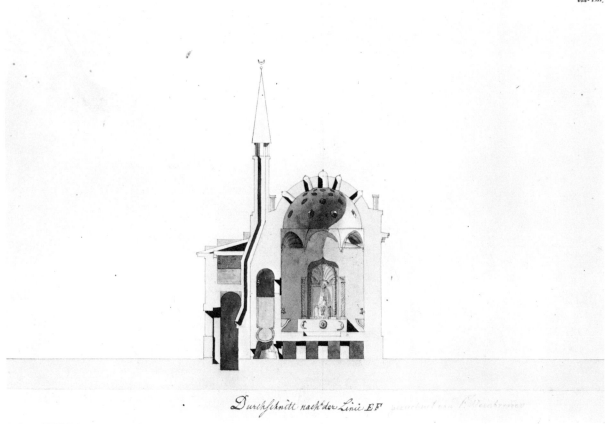

Durchschnitt nach der Linie EF

59

The whimsical design is a combination of two Ottoman building types: the mosque and the *hamman* (bath). The central chamber, covered by a coffered and perforated dome, is built over a hypocaust in the Roman fashion. The details, however, are Oriental, including an astonishing minaret-shaped chimney.

Weinbrenner's interest in baths can be traced back to his student days, when he drew extraordinary reconstructions of the Baths of Hippias in Rome and the Roman baths in Baden-weiler, not far from Baden-Baden. For his exotic Turkish design Weinbrenner must have consulted Aubry de La Mottraye's *Travels Through Europe, Asia and into Parts of Africa* (London, 1723), with etchings by William Hogarth, in which there is a view of a Turkish bath interior and illustrations of other landmarks in Constantinople. Weinbrenner captured the essential contemplative atmosphere if not the actual form of the *hamman*, a far smaller bath than its grandiose Roman predecessors. *R. W.*

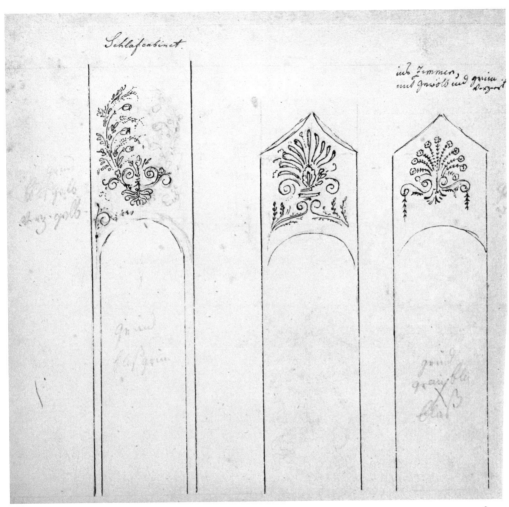

61

60–67 (218.11, 218.4–218.9, 218.3v)
GRAND DUCAL PALACE,
KARLSRUHE
Friedrich Weinbrenner, architect

Weinbrenner was responsible for several campaigns of refitting and modernizing the interiors of the eighteenth-century Grand Ducal Pal-ace, the most important of which occurred early in the reign of Grand Duke Karl and Grand Duchess Steph-anie (1811–18). Cat. 60 is his plan for the grand duchess's private apart-ments, located on the ground floor in the northwest pavilion of the palace (see figs. 7 and 8). Her suite, which overlooked the gardens, comprised a blue wallpapered oval drawing room, flanked by a billiard room at left and a yellow cabinet at right. A library called the Grau Salon, to the lower right of the oval salon, was an espe-cially fine example of Weinbrenner's disciplined taste for the antique (see fig. 9).

Stephanie was Napoleon's adopted daughter, and her patronage re-inforced the already established

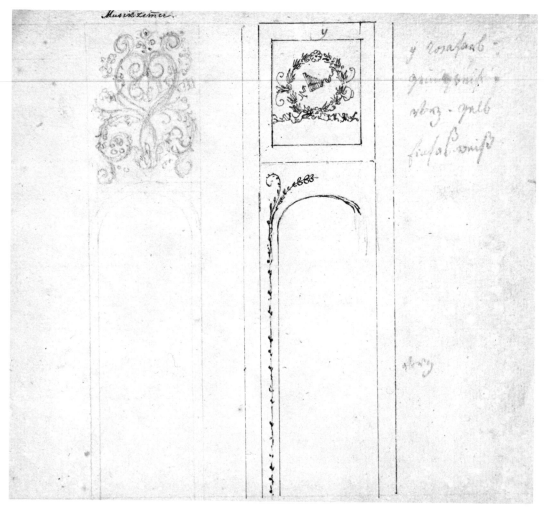

62

Empire Style in Karlsruhe. What is probably a design for the bed canopy in her state bedroom (cat. 67) bears comparison with contemporary work in Paris. However, echoes from the older components of international neoclassicism continued to be heard. For example, the spidery embroidery of the ceiling in the billiard room (cat. 60 left) was derived from the architecture of Robert Adam, perhaps filtered through the work of Percier and Fontaine. The rectangular paneling designed for what was probably the grand duke's private bedroom (cat. 61), the music room (cat. 62), and several rooms for the grand duke and duchess (cats. 63, 64) recalls the earlier, antirococo classicism of Claude-Nicolas Ledoux.

Although Weinbrenner's architectural vocabulary was restrained, his palette was bright and varied. The right border of cat. 63 bears his color specifications, including yellow, orange, red, violet, and green. A yellow-gold molding detail for the grand duchess's reception room and bedroom (cat. 65) further exemplifies his taste.

That antique precedents lay behind such work is demonstrated by the lively frieze invented for the grand

63

duke's room (cat. 66). The same combination of couchant griffins and vine tendrils appears frequently in Roman fourth-style wall painting, such as Weinbrenner would have seen in the Domus Aurea in Rome or at Herculaneum and Pompeii. Griffins were an especially appropriate subject, for one figured in the coat of arms of Baden, but they were also popular with Percier and Fontaine.

BIBLIOGRAPHY

Gutman 1911, 51–52; Schneider 1961; Stratmann 1980 and 1976 (2d ed., 1982, 14, 17); Valdenaire 1919 (2d ed., 1926, 101).

65

66

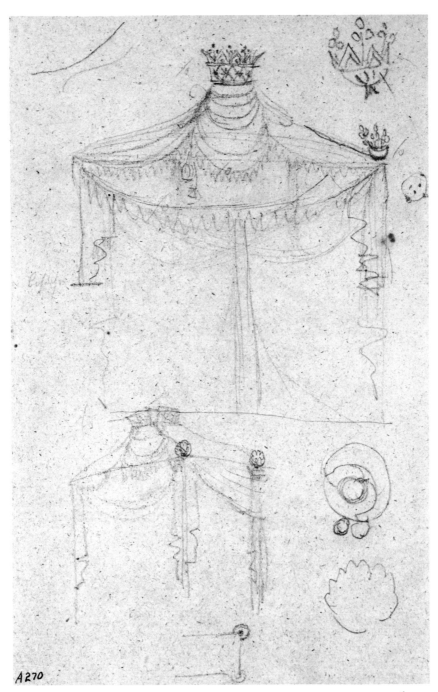

A270

A238

68

68 (210.14v)
CEILING DESIGN WITH SWANS
School of Weinbrenner

Weinbrenner's love of ancient ornament is also apparent in this ceiling
panel, divided into triangular sections

with a rosette boss. In the panels a
swan with spread wings perches on
a vine whose leaves curl into volutes.
This motif closely emulates the decorative frieze of the Ara Pacis, the
Roman monument that honored Au-
gustus's pacification of Spain and

Gaul. During Weinbrenner's stay in
Italy, the Ara Pacis had been a favorite
object of study. In classical literature
swans were considered great music
lovers, for they sang beautifully at the
moment of their death; this ceiling
may thus have been intended for the

69

Grand Ducal Palace's music room or theater, or for one of the public theaters that Weinbrenner designed. *L. B.*

BIBLIOGRAPHY

Weinbrenner 1958, 198.

69 (236.1)
STENCIL FOR PALMETTE

This stencil demonstrates Weinbrenner's method for repeating a decorative motif with exactitude throughout a room or suite of rooms. The template was traced on a wall and specified colors were then added. The stencil, which records half a design, must be flipped over to create the whole motif. The leaves with curled tips resemble the beloved classical anthemion. *L. B.*

70 (223.1r)
KATHOLISCHE STADTKIRCHE, KARLSRUHE
School of Weinbrenner

This drawing of vine ornament for the dome of the Katholische Stadtkirche records a little-known phase of that church's interior decoration. Construction of the centrally planned building began in 1808, and Weinbrenner's original proposal for the interior of the dome comprised an umbrella of radiating segments, filled with grotesque ornament and divided into horizontal registers, in the lowest of which stood a row of angels. This scheme, however, was rejected by the client because it contained too many secular images of plants and animals. The dome was apparently undecorated when the church was dedicated to St. Stephan on December 26, 1814, and in 1817 and 1818, when structural problems in the dome necessitated the repainting of the interior, Josef Sandhaas was commissioned to decorate the vault with stars. Dated 1823, the Pennsylvania drawing documents the subsequent removal of the dome's star-studded decoration and the transformation of the interior to something like the appearance proposed at the time of the church's completion, albeit without angels. The design is closely modeled on the painted semidome in room 85 of the Domus Aurea in Rome. An 1882 rebuilding substituted illusionistic coffers for what is seen here. *L. B.*

BIBLIOGRAPHY

Geier n.d.; Staatliche Kunsthalle 1977, 63–65; Valdenaire 1919 (2d ed., 1926, 277–82).

70

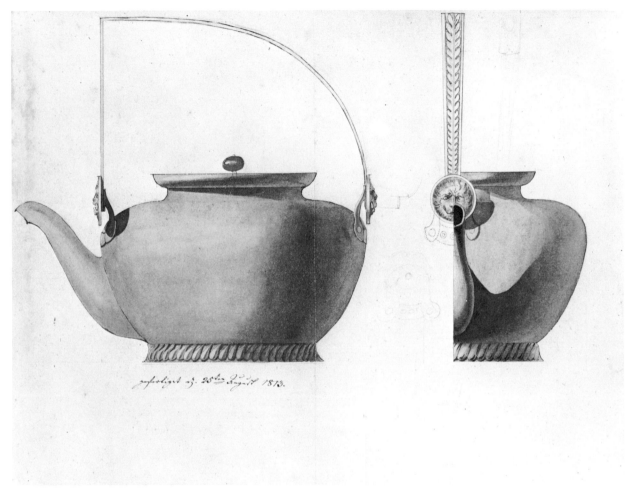

71

71 (234.1)
TEAPOT
School of Weinbrenner

One of the most beautiful drawings in the collection, this work of August 25, 1813, expresses Weinbrenner's refreshing approach to the antique. The sharp contours of the teapot, which are emphasized by the drawing's strongly contrasting highlights and shadows, give it a stark and quasi-modern appearance. But while the drawing seems to herald the design of the twentieth century, it is still a product of that early nineteenth-century enthusiasm for antiquity that Weinbrenner epitomized. This phenomenon was complex. Although the lion-headed boss at the handle attachment finds many precedents on ancient vessels, the simple body of the kettle is a more generalized interpretation of ancient forms. It is this mixture of knowledgeable emulation and abstraction that gives the object its retrospective and prospective character. *L. B.*

BIBLIOGRAPHY

Lankheit 1976, 12, 13 (ill.).

72

72 (224.1)
LIVING ROOM OF THE
PRINCESS OF ORANIEN,
BADEN-BADEN (?)

Dated 1835, nine years after Weinbrenner's death, this drawing shows the
subsequent transformation of classical
taste in Baden. The drawing's inscription reads: "The living room of her
highness the Princess of Oranien
during her visit to Baden. / Drawn for
her highness the Grand Duchess of
Baden for the album in which the
princess of the same preserves her
keepsakes." The princess of Oranien

was Frederica-Louisa Wilhelmina
(1774–1837), the wife of William I
of the Netherlands (1772–1844). Her
living room is shown crowded with
chairs, tables, and sofas, and the walls
are covered with pictures. The cozi-
ness conveyed by this multiplicity
of furnishings characterizes the Biedermeier style, the German and
Austrian successor to the classicism
practiced by Weinbrenner and his
contemporaries.

Biedermeier was not a rejection of
classicism but a simpler interpretation
of the same themes. Furniture forms
were reduced to a basic geometry that

was slightly softened by curves, while
decoration was virtually eliminated.
The princess's living room includes
examples of typical Biedermeier furniture types and arrangements. The
chair in the foreground, with its saber
legs and pierced three-reed splat, was
popular in the period. The Biedermeier manner of living stressed the
home, and the different kinds of tables
shown here, as well as their placement, would have established separate
islands of activity within this domestic
center. Such simple furniture was
greatly admired by Josef Hoffmann
and Adolf Loos, the leading modern-

73

ists of turn-of-the-century Vienna.
L. B.

BIBLIOGRAPHY

Georg Himmelheber, *Biedermeier Furniture*, trans. and ed. Simon Jervis (London: Faber and Faber, 1974), 29, 36–45; Mara Reissberger and Peter Haiko, "Alles ist einfach und glatt: Zur Dialektik der Ornamentlosigkeit," in *Moderne Vergangenheit, 1800–1900* (Vienna: Künstlerhaus, 1981), 13–19.

73–79 (194.12, 194.11, 194.8, 194.10, 194.9, 194.4, 194.7)
WEINBRENNER'S *ARCHITEKTONISCHES LEHRBUCH*

The first fascicle of Friedrich Weinbrenner's *Architektonisches Lehrbuch* appeared in 1810. Its four projected volumes were to explore the entire range of architecture, from drafting and construction to architectural history and theory. But while three volumes had been issued by the time of Weinbrenner's death in 1826, the fourth volume, already in manuscript, was never printed. Thus left incomplete (and quite rare), the *Lehrbuch* nevertheless exerted important influence as Germany's first comprehensive manual on the theory and practice of architecture. It played a role, as did Weinbrenner's own architectural school, in establishing an academic architectural tradition in Germany that

74

was no longer entirely dependent on France and Italy.

The first two volumes of the *Lehrbuch* deal exclusively with drawing, and the student is given increasingly complicated perspective problems to solve. In the advanced exercises the student learns to construct drawings with several vanishing points, such as views up and down stairs require (cats. 73–75). These carefully rendered wash drawings,

almost certainly executed by one of Weinbrenner's office draftsmen, never appeared in this form in the *Lehrbuch*. As explained in his preface, Weinbrenner had hoped to include tinted illustrations, but such reproductions proved too costly; Weinbrenner was thus forced to use lithographs, for which ink preparatory drawings were submitted. The view up the stairs shows this revision: The wash drawing (cat. 75) was remade as a line drawing

(cat. 76), which was then printed, with the figural entourage again revised (cat. 77).

Created solely as drawing problems and not representing any known Weinbrenner buildings, the simple subjects of these perspective studies are nevertheless given great dignity. The same auxiliary lines that define the perspective also establish the axial order that governs and monumentalizes the architecture.

75

Long before readers of the *Lehrbuch* encounter even such simple architectural subjects, they have been shown how to construct and manipulate plane and simple figures. An illustration from the second volume (cat. 78) shows a typical lesson in rendering irregular plane figures in perspective; once again, the wash colors added by draftsman Friedrich Arnold were omitted in the published *Lehrbuch*. By the time the classical orders are taught, students who had followed this course of study would have developed a keen appreciation of the platonic geometric solids out of which capitals, metopes, and triglyphs are assembled (cat. 79). When this is mastered Weinbrenner introduces the drawing of entire buildings, choosing many of his own Karlsruhe works for examples. Young architects who finished the course presented in the first two volumes of the *Lehrbuch* would thus have done more than master technical drawing and learn the hierarchical relationship between the elements of classical architecture; they would also have been inoculated—without ever having read a word of architectural theory—with the stereometry of Weinbrenner's personal style. *M. J. L.*

BIBLIOGRAPHY

Lankheit 1976, 25–34.

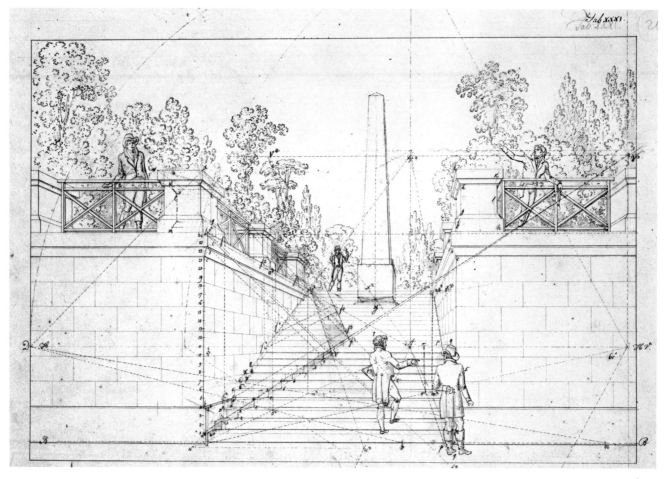

Tab. XXXI.

Weinbrenners Lehrbuch 2ᵗᵉ Th. 6t Hft.

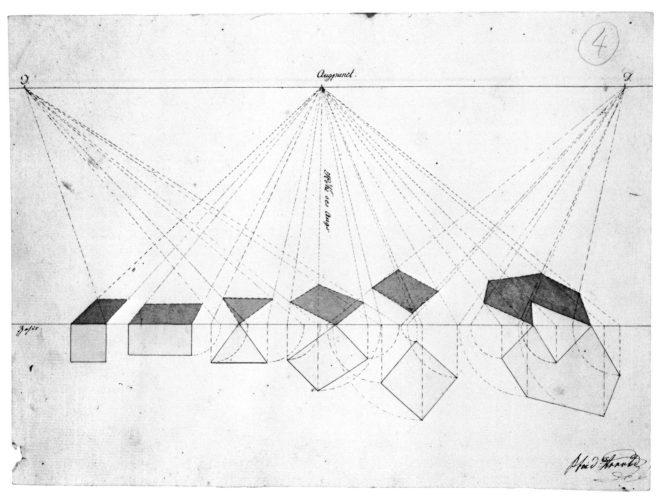

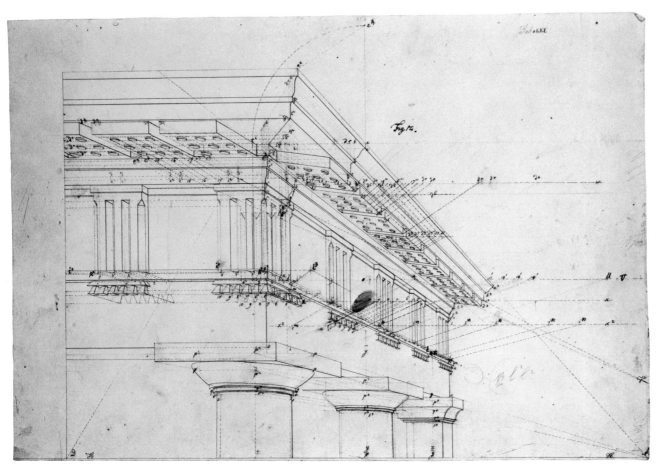

80 (200.1)
DETAILS AND ELEVATIONS OF PALLADIAN BUILDINGS
School of Weinbrenner

Weinbrenner's debt to Italian Renaissance architect Andrea Palladio (1508–1580) was profound, and there is evidence of it even in his earliest student works. For Weinbrenner this style and the rediscovered architecture of Greece were the two acceptable variants of classicism; he called them the Palladian and the Paestum styles, and he mixed them in his designs with surprising freedom. In view of this, it is remarkable that although he visited Paestum during his five-year residence in Italy, he never visited Vicenza, where nearly all Palladio's great works are located. Palladio, it seems, could be mastered from books.

These renderings, apparently the work of one of Weinbrenner's students, document the continuing interest in Palladio among Weinbrenner's circle and demonstrate the manner in which he was studied. The large sheet is entirely devoted to the urban *palazzi* and country villas of Palladio. The first column on the left contains, from top to bottom, the Porto al Castello, the Palazzo Thiene, a probable detail of the Porto al Castello, and the Palazzo Porto. The second column contains the Villa Pisani, the Palazzo Cogollo, and the Capitaniato Loggia. The two orders in the upper right appear to be the Ionic and Doric orders of the Villa Pisani; below these are the Palazzo Civena on the right and the Villa Rotunda. The first two drawings in the lower left depict the Palazzo Chiericati and the Palazzo Thiene al Castello.

These drawings are not travel documents and appear instead to be based on engravings of Palladio's work. The facade of the Capitaniato Loggia, for example, does not seem to have been drawn from the existing brick facade, but from the ennobled version published in Francesco Muttoni's *Architettura di Andrea Palladio* (Venice, 1740–48). The size and format of the drawings themselves resemble the plates in Ottavio Bertotti Scamozzi's *Les batimens et les desseins de André Palladio* (Vicenza, 1776–83), an accessible recent edition that Weinbrenner might have acquired during his Italian years.

While not included in Weinbrenner's *Architektonisches Lehrbuch*, this sheet nonetheless appears to have been intended for publication. The subject was probably not Palladian buildings, but the Palladian proportions on which they were based. Elements such as capitals and carved ornament are drawn sketchily or not at all; whole buildings are not shown, but only enough to indicate the articulation of each bay. Even the unmistakable Villa Rotunda is represented by a strangely disjointed sliver.

Weinbrenner's own Palladian works are derived from the Renaissance architect's country villas and never from his highly mannered town houses. It was the country houses that satisfied the taste of Weinbrenner's generation for sheer expanses of wall surface and the massing of simple cubical volumes. *M. J. L.*

BIBLIOGRAPHY

Everke 1981, 44–64.

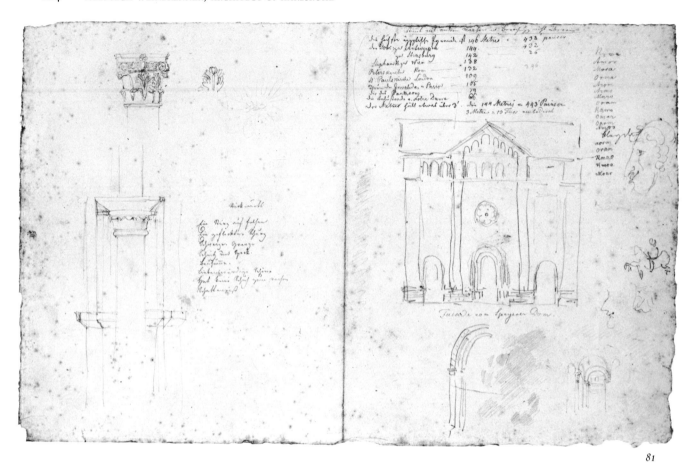

81

81, 82 (196.1, 196.2)
STUDIES OF SPEYER
CATHEDRAL
School of Weinbrenner

Along with Berlin architects David
Gilly, Friedrich Gilly, and Karl Friedrich Schinkel, Friedrich Weinbrenner
was among the first German architects
to turn to Germany's medieval past as
a subject for scholarly study and a
source of inspiration. Some of Weinbrenner's designs, such as the Gothic
tower on the Countess Amalie's estate

in Karlsruhe, recalled the older tradition of exotic garden "follies," where
the Gothic style had roughly the same
exotic cachet as Chinese architecture.
On the other hand, a project such as
Weinbrenner's rebuilding of the medieval castle at Neu-Eberstein was an
actual, if inaccurate, restoration of
a building in its original style.

These two drawings document the
involvement of Weinbrenner's circle
with one of medieval Germany's most
important monuments, Speyer Cathedral. Begun in the early eleventh
century but not consecrated until

1125, the cathedral is among the most
important Romanesque churches in
the Rhineland. Dated March 1826, the
drawings range in precision of execution from the scrupulously rendered
capital of the choir arcade to the
sketchy treatment of the facade. Apparently part of an architect's portfolio
of travel sketches and intended for his
personal use, the drawings show a
number of playful digressions; to the
right of the facade is a list of all the
permutations of the letters "Roma,
Amor," and so forth, while beneath
these a caricature suggests the jowly

profile of Weinbrenner himself, who had died two months earlier.

Most remarkable is the elevation of the facade, consisting of a triple portal whose bays are divided by strip buttresses and whose central gable has a corbel frieze. Convincingly Romanesque, the drawing nevertheless depicts neither the original medieval facade, which had been destroyed during the sixteenth century, nor the facade the delineator would have seen in 1826: Balthasar Neuman's medieval fantasy of the 1770s, with its traceried round arches and corner obelisks. While the other studies and details of the building appear to represent the existing building, the facade therefore appears to be a conjectural restoration. It strongly resembles the neo-Romanesque facade given to the cathedral between 1854 and 1858, when the restoration architect was Heinrich Hübsch, a pupil of Weinbrenner. These drawings suggest that his work was indebted to an investigation of Speyer Cathedral that began in the mid-1820s in Weinbrenner's circle. *M. J. L.*

BIBLIOGRAPHY

Hans Erich Kubach and Walter Haas, *Der Dom zu Speyer*, 3 vols. (Munich: Deutscher Kunstverlag, 1972).

83 (198.1)
ROMANESQUE ARCH FORMS
School of Weinbrenner

Weinbrenner's influence was disseminated across Germany not only through his *Architektonisches Lehrbuch* and other published writings, but also through his private architectural school and by the young architects he trained. While the older of these, including Georg Moller, seldom escaped the legacy of Weinbrenner's classicism, the next generation of pupils was designing very different-looking buildings within a few years of their mentor's death. These architects, belonging to the generation born around 1800, worked in a mode distinguished by its round-arched masonry construction and an ornamental vocabulary based on Romanesque, Byzantine, and early Renaissance detail. Weinbrenner pupils carried this style to northern German cities such as Hamburg (Alexis de Chateauneuf) and Hanover (August Andreae), while it was represented in Karlsruhe by Heinrich Hübsch; it was this last-mentioned architect who defined this new style and named it "Rundbogenstil" in his 1828 manifesto *In welchem Style sollen wir bauen?*.

In its pragmatic emphasis on the specifics of construction and materials, the Rundbogenstil reflected notions that had already been stressed in Weinbrenner's protomaterialist teaching. Originally used to justify the details of Greek architecture, Weinbrenner had increasingly broadened the argument of material determinism to explain medieval architecture as well. This sketch (cat. 83) is an important document of the way in which medieval architecture was thus systematically studied in Weinbrenner's circle; it is part of a portfolio of drawings of Romanesque buildings. Instead of depicting the measured fragments of visited buildings, the sheet is a typological survey of round-arched forms and shows the increasing elaboration of grouped, cusped, and intersecting arches that can be derived from the basic constructional unit of the round arch.

The sheet is headed "Byzantinisch, romanisch, vorgothisch" and reflects the confusion of terms surrounding the Romanesque, which in the 1820s was only beginning to be understood as a style distinct from the Gothic. Significantly, it was Moller whose *Denkmäler der deutschen Baukunst* provided the first comprehensive study of the style. Cat. 83 links Moller's scholarly studies and Hübsch's new style to Weinbrenner's lectures on architectural history. *M. J. L.*

BIBLIOGRAPHY

Heinrich Hübsch, *In welchem Style sollen wir bauen?* (Karlsruhe: C. F. Müller, 1828).

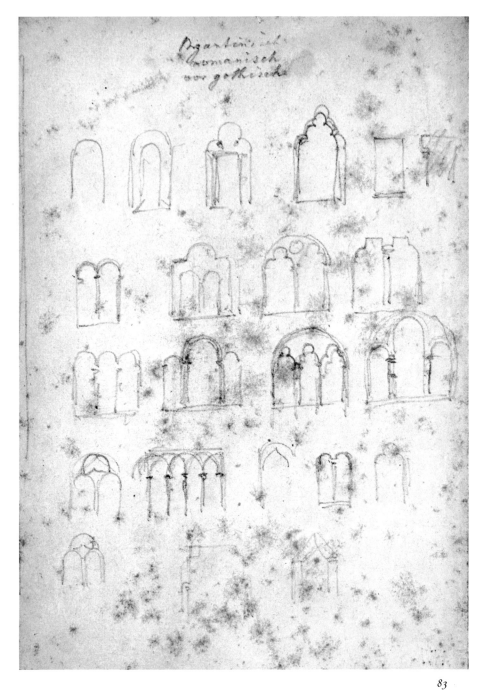

84

84 (206.1r)
FOUR MEDIEVAL STAGE SETS (?)
Friedrich Gilly (?)

Although Friedrich Weinbrenner visited Berlin in 1792, he never acknowledged his acquaintance with David Gilly (1748–1808) or David's tragically short-lived son Friedrich (1772–1800), the most notable Prussian architects of that era. The Philadelphia collection convincingly demonstrates, however, that Weinbrenner's designs for garden buildings (cat. 20) and farms (cat. 32) were profoundly indebted to the work of those Berliners; moreover, the inclusion in the collection of this sheet of sketches, apparently drawn by Friedrich Gilly himself, indicates that Weinbrenner's association with them was both deep and personal.

The four illustrated interiors are all medieval in detail, conceived under the spell that Marienburg Castle had cast over the younger Gilly when he surveyed it in 1794, the first respectful visit paid by a modern German architect to a Gothic site. The drawings are not of the castle itself, however; instead, they resemble the medieval stage sets that Gilly often recorded or invented in subsequent years. They may well date from his Parisian sojourn in the second half of 1797, which he devoted largely to the examination of theaters.

The dramatically shadowed silhouettes of the vignette at upper left—a view into an interior courtyard—are characteristic of one aspect of the Gilly style; typical of another is the fluent, heavy-lined technique used for the large sketch at lower left, showing a vaulted stairhall in which a Piranesian chain hangs from a pier. The tiny views at right—a crypt (top) and another courtyard (bottom)—are drawn in his linear style with coarse vigor, and they also betray Gilly's inclination to reduce Gothic arches to simple triangular forms. His habit of rendering medieval and all other structural systems in their simplest geometry has often been seen as a presentiment of modernist ideology.

Friedrich Gilly's distinctive sketching was widely celebrated and much copied. His student Karl Friedrich Schinkel was an especially enthusiastic copyist, as was the painter Carl Wilhelm Kolbe (1781–1853). The drawing in question may be a copy by an admirer, but Dr. Hella Reelfs, who has successfully sorted out the Gilly copyists, believes that it is probably an original. How it came to Karlsruhe is difficult to reconstruct, for it dates after Weinbrenner's only visit to Berlin, and it is not recorded that Gilly ever passed through Baden. What is certain, however, is that the presence of such a sheet in a collection of Weinbrenner drawings demonstrates a heretofore neglected artistic connection between Berlin and Karlsruhe. *D. B.*

BIBLIOGRAPHY

Berlin Museum, *Friedrich Gilly, 1772–1800, und die Privatgesellschaft junger Architekten* (Berlin: Willmuth Arenhövel, 1984); assistance from Hella Reelfs.

Checklist of the
Weinbrenner Collection in the
Architectural Archives of the
University of Pennsylvania

Note: Drawings marked with an asterisk (*) are illustrated and discussed in this catalogue.

2 VILLA AND ESTATE OF MARGRAVINE
CHRISTIANE LOUISE, KARLSRUHE
Friedrich Weinbrenner, architect
See cats. 1–8 for project description

*2.1 VILLA: NORTH AND SOUTH
ELEVATIONS, GROUND AND FIRST
FLOOR ABOVE GROUND PLANS,
AND TRANSVERSE SECTION (cat. 1)
Ink, graphite, watercolor, and wash on laid
paper
45 × 73 cm
c. 1817

*2.2 VILLA: WEST ELEVATION (cat. 2)
Ink, watercolor, and wash on laid paper
30.5 × 49.5 cm
c. 1817

2.3 VILLA: FIRST FLOOR ABOVE
GROUND PLAN
Ink, graphite, and wash on laid paper
36 × 51.5 cm
c. 1821, possibly preparatory to the first
volume of Weinbrenner's *Gebäude*
(1822–35) but marked with different plate
numbers

*2.4 VILLA: NORTH ELEVATION (recto)
GENERAL VIEW OF ESTATE FROM
SOUTH (verso) (cat. 3)
Ink, graphite, watercolor, and wash on laid
paper

37 × 51.5 cm
c. 1821, possibly preparatory to the first
volume of Weinbrenner's *Gebäude*
(1822–35) but marked with different plate
numbers

2.5 VILLA: SOUTH ELEVATION
Ink, graphite, watercolor, and wash on laid
paper
36.5 × 51.5 cm
c. 1821, possibly preparatory to the first
volume of Weinbrenner's *Gebäude*
(1822–35) but marked with different plate
numbers

2.6 VILLA: EAST ELEVATION
Ink, graphite, watercolor, and wash on laid
paper
36.5 × 50 cm
c. 1821, possibly preparatory to the first
volume of Weinbrenner's *Gebäude*
(1822–35) but marked with different plate
numbers

2.7 VILLA: TRANSVERSE SECTION
Ink, graphite, watercolor, and wash on laid
paper
36.5 × 51.5 cm
c. 1821, possibly preparatory to the first
volume of Weinbrenner's *Gebäude*
(1822–35) but marked with different plate
numbers

2.8 GARDEN HOUSE: NORTH ELEVATION
Ink and graphite on laid paper
31 × 46 cm

c. 1821, possibly preparatory to the first
volume of Weinbrenner's *Gebäude*
(1822–35)

2.9 GARDEN HOUSE: NORTH ELEVATION
Ink and graphite on tracing paper mounted
on laid paper
25 × 42.5 cm (mount)
Possibly a later copy of 2.8

*2.10 GARDEN HOUSE: SOUTH ELEVATION
(*cat. 4*)
Ink, watercolor, and wash on tracing paper
mounted on laid paper
20.5 × 40 cm (mount)
Copy of drawing that possibly was
preparatory to the first volume of
Weinbrenner's *Gebäude* (1822–35)

2.11 GARDEN HOUSE: FIRST FLOOR
ABOVE GROUND PLAN
Ink and wash on tracing paper mounted on
laid paper
22 × 39 cm (mount)
Copy of drawing that possibly was
preparatory to the first volume of
Weinbrenner's *Gebäude* (1822–35)

*2.12 PLANT HOUSE: PLAN, SOUTH
ELEVATION, AND TRANSVERSE
SECTION (*cat. 6*)
Ink, graphite, watercolor, and wash on laid
paper
36 × 52 cm
c. 1817

*2.13 VEGETABLE GARDEN GATEWAY: PLAN
AND NORTH, SOUTH, AND EAST
ELEVATIONS (*cat. 7*)
Graphite on laid paper
34.5 × 31 cm
Signed and dated "Genehmiget/den 28ten
Marz/1818/Christiane Luise verw. Mrg
zu Baden"

*2.14 ARBOR: PLAN AND WEST ELEVATION
(*cat. 5*)
Ink, graphite, watercolor, and wash on laid
paper

31 × 46.5 cm
Signed and dated "Genehmiget den
11ten/April 1818/Christiane Luise/verw.
Mrg. zu Baden"

*2.15 STABLE AND GARDENER'S HOUSE:
WEST AND SOUTH ELEVATIONS
(*cat. 8*)
Ink and graphite on tracing paper mounted
on wove paper
37 × 31.5 cm (mount)
Copy of drawing that possibly was
preparatory to the first volume of
Weinbrenner's *Gebäude* (1822–35)

2.16 STABLE AND GARDENER'S HOUSE:
GROUND PLAN
Ink and wash on tracing paper mounted on
laid paper
18.5 × 30 cm (mount)
Copy of drawing that possibly was
preparatory to the first volume of
Weinbrenner's *Gebäude* (1822–35)

4 VILLA AND ESTATE OF MARGRAVINE
AMALIE, KARLSRUHE
Friedrich Weinbrenner, architect
See cats. 9, 10 for project description

*4.1 SITE PLAN (*cat. 9*)
Ink and watercolor on laid paper
13 × 27.5 cm
c. 1806, preparatory to a similarly oriented
engraving of the site plan (recorded by
Landesdenkmalamt K624)

*4.2 VILLA: GROUND PLAN AND WEST
ELEVATION (*cat. 10*)
Ink, graphite, watercolor, and wash on laid
paper
42 × 30 cm
c. 1821, possibly preparatory to the second
volume of Weinbrenner's *Gebäude*
(1822–35)

4.3 VILLA: MEZZANINE PLAN AND EAST
ELEVATION

Ink, graphite, watercolor, and wash on laid
paper
42 × 30.5 cm
c. 1821, possibly preparatory to the second
volume of Weinbrenner's *Gebäude*
(1822–35)

4.4 VILLA: WEST ELEVATION AND
TRANSVERSE SECTION
Ink, graphite, and watercolor on laid paper
43 × 28.5 cm
c. 1821, possibly preparatory to the second
volume of Weinbrenner's *Gebäude*
(1822–35)

4.5 VILLA: SOUTH ELEVATION AND
LONGITUDINAL SECTION
Ink, graphite, and watercolor on laid paper
43 × 28.5 cm
c. 1821, possibly preparatory to the second
volume of Weinbrenner's *Gebäude*
(1822–35)

6 MARGRAVES' ESTATE, KARLSRUHE
Friedrich Weinbrenner, architect
See cats. 11–14 for project description

6.1 GARDEN HOUSE, VERSION 1: PLAN
AND NORTH ELEVATION
Ink and watercolor on laid paper
48.5 × 31 cm
Signed and dated on verso "Carlsruh . . . /d.
3 Juny 1812 Th[ierry]"

*6.2 GARDEN HOUSE, VERSION 2: PLAN
AND NORTH ELEVATION *(cat. 12)*
Ink, watercolor, and wash on laid paper
52 × 31 cm
Signed and dated on verso "Carlsruh den
5ten Juli . . . /1811 Thierry"

*6.3 GARDEN HOUSE, VERSION 2:
TRANSVERSE AND LONGITUDINAL
SECTIONS *(cat. 13)*
Ink and watercolor on laid paper
46.5 × 31 cm
c. 1811

6.4 GARDEN HOUSE, VERSION 2:
TRANSVERSE AND LONGITUDINAL
SECTIONS
Ink, graphite, and watercolor on laid paper
52 × 31 cm
Signed and dated on verso "Carlsruh den 7tn
July 1811/Thierry"

*6.5 GARDEN HOUSE, VERSION 3: NORTH
AND SOUTH ELEVATIONS *(cat. 14)*
Ink and watercolor on laid paper
43.5 × 31.5 cm
c. 1811

*6.6 STABLE ADDITION FOR TWENTY-SIX
HORSES: GROUND PLAN, NORTH
AND WEST ELEVATIONS, AND
TRANSVERSE SECTION *(cat. 11)*
Ink, graphite, watercolor, and wash on laid
paper
64.5 × 45 cm
c. 1813
Signed "F. Weinbrenner"

8 GARDEN HOUSE WITH ARBOR,
QUERALLEE, KARLSRUHE
School of Weinbrenner
See cat. 21 for project description

*8.1 GROUND FLOOR PLAN, GARDEN
ELEVATION, AND TRANSVERSE AND
LONGITUDINAL SECTIONS *(cat. 21)*
Ink, watercolor, and wash on laid paper
32 × 27 cm
c. 1805
Signed "Ж"

10 PALLADIAN GARDEN HOUSE,
QUERALLEE, KARLSRUHE
Friedrich Weinbrenner or Ferdinand
Thierry (?), architect
Mounted on a tall, rusticated basement,
this porticoed project is identified by an in-
scription as intended for the Querallee (now
Zähringerstrasse) *(see cat. 21)*

10.1 PLAN AND NORTH AND SOUTH
ELEVATIONS
Ink, watercolor, and wash on laid paper
46.5 × 27.5 cm
Drawn by Ferdinand Thierry (?) c. 1805

12 PALLADIAN GARDEN HOUSE,
KARLSRUHE
Friedrich Weinbrenner or Ferdinand (?)
Thierry, architect
This astylar, two-story project seems related to
10.1 and may be for the same site

12.1 FRONT AND REAR ELEVATIONS
Ink, watercolor, and wash on laid paper
49 × 31.5 cm
Signed and dated "Carls. den 25ten Marz
1812/Thierry"

14 GARDEN HOUSE WITH DORIC
ENTABLATURE, COBURG(?)
Friedrich Weinbrenner or Karl Thierry,
architect
Small but formal C-plan project, one story tall,
designed in Coburg, near the Thuringian area
where Wilhelm and Ferdinand Thierry were
active

14.1 PLAN AND FRONT ELEVATION
Ink, watercolor, and wash on wove paper
32 × 19 cm
Signed and dated "Thierry/gez. in Coburg,
July [18]21"

14.2 REAR AND SIDE ELEVATIONS
Ink, watercolor, and wash on wove paper
32 × 19 cm
Signed and dated "C. Thierry/July. 1821"

16 TROPICAL GARDEN HOUSE
(UNIDENTIFIED)
Crude but vigorous project for a square build-
ing on a tall, rusticated basement, with its roof

peak crowned by a tuft of palm leaves; 16.2
adds a Doric porch and pilasters, adopting the
suggestion given by a pencil elevation on 16.1

16.1 VERSION 1: PLAN AND FOUR
ELEVATIONS
Ink and graphite on laid paper
22 × 35 cm
c. 1810 (?)

16.2 VERSION 2: PLAN AND THREE
ELEVATIONS
Ink and graphite on laid paper
29.5 × 35 cm
c. 1810 (?)

18 ROMAN HOUSE, ROTENFELS
Friedrich Weinbrenner, architect
See cat. 18 for project description

*18.1 PRELIMINARY NORTH AND EAST
ELEVATIONS (*cat. 18*)
Ink and watercolor on laid paper
19 × 51.5 cm
c. 1808

18.2 PRELIMINARY NORTH AND EAST
ELEVATIONS AND PLAN
Graphite on laid paper
21 × 35 cm

20 PORTICOED GARDEN HOUSE,
BADENWEILER (?)
Friedrich Weinbrenner, architect
The two versions of this project for a small
Doric building vary only in proportions; tenta-
tively identified with the design of c. 1811 for
Badenweiler on the basis of Stadtarchiv XV
1264 (20.1 is labeled in French)

20.1 VERSION 1: SIDE ELEVATION AND
LONGITUDINAL SECTION
Ink, watercolor, and wash on laid paper
46.5 × 31 cm
c. 1811–12

20.2 VERSION 2: PLAN, FRONT AND SIDE
ELEVATIONS, AND LONGITUDINAL
SECTION
Ink, watercolor, and wash on laid paper
51.5 × 36 cm
Signed and dated on verso "Carls den 6tcn
Juny 1812/Thierry"

24 THATCHED PAVILION FOR PRINCE
PUTIATIN, SCHACKWITZ
Friedrich Weinbrenner, architect
See cat. 20 for project description

*24.1 PLAN, TWO ELEVATIONS,
TRANSVERSE SECTION, AND TWO
DETAILS *(cat. 20)*
Ink and watercolor on wove paper
28.5 × 46.5 cm
Watermark "1794/J WHATMAN"

26 GARDENER'S HOUSE WITH BRIDGE
(UNIDENTIFIED)
School of Weinbrenner (Miessel?)
See cat. 19 for project description

*26.1 ELEVATION *(cat. 19)*
Ink and watercolor on laid paper
25 × 43.5 cm
c. 1815

28 GARDEN TEMPLE FOR THE DUKE OF
GOTHA
Friedrich Weinbrenner, architect
Distyle in antis at both ends of a mirrored hex-
agonal cella; identified in Geier sketchbook

28.1 PLAN
Graphite on wove paper
48.5 × 31 cm
Watermark "Ruse & Turners/1805"

30 DISTYLE-IN-ANTIS GARDEN TEMPLE,
KARLSRUHE
Friedrich Weinbrenner or Ferdinand (?)
Thierry, architect

Small, sober building with Doric columns at
each end, sheltering two facing benches; plan
resembles that of the ruined temple that stood
in the Grand Ducal Palace's pheasantry garden

30.1 PLAN AND FRONT ELEVATION
Ink, watercolor, and wash on laid paper
61.5 × 45 cm
Signed and dated on verso "Carlsruh den
12ten August 1810/Thierry"

30.2 SIDE ELEVATION
Ink, watercolor, and wash on laid paper
46.5 × 31 cm
Signed and dated on verso "Carlsruh den
23ten Augst 1810/Thierry"

30.3 LONGITUDINAL SECTION
Ink, watercolor, and wash on laid paper
46.5 × 31 cm
Drawn by Ferdinand Thierry (?) c. 1810

32 RUINED GARDEN TEMPLE,
KARLSRUHE (?)
Friedrich Weinbrenner or Miessel, architect (?)
See cat. 17 for project description

*32.1 FRONT ELEVATION *(cat. 17)*
Ink, watercolor, and wash on laid paper
26.5 × 41.5 cm
c. 1815
Signed "Michel"

34 PLANT HOUSE, BOTANICAL GARDEN,
KARLSRUHE
Friedrich Weinbrenner, architect
See cat. 15 for project description

*34.1 SOUTH AND EAST ELEVATIONS
(cat. 15)
Ink, watercolor, and wash on laid paper
31 × 46.5 cm
c. 1808

36 PLANT HOUSE, BRUCHSAL
Friedrich Weinbrenner, architect (?)
See cat. 16 for project description

*36.1 TRANSVERSE SECTION AND PLAN
(cat. 16)
Ink, watercolor, and wash on laid paper
37 × 51.5 cm
c. 1810 (?)

38 ARBOR (UNIDENTIFIED)
School of Weinbrenner
Semicircular in plan, with Ionic pilasters; alternative curved and peaked roofs shown

38.1 PLAN AND FRONT ELEVATION
Ink, watercolor, and wash on laid paper
45 × 31 cm
c. 1810

40 CHINESE PAVILION, KARLSRUHE (?)
F (?), architect
Drawing shows the mechanism for opening the roof of a Chinese pavilion, of which Karlsruhe had many: two small buildings erected by Friedrich von Kesslau in the palace pheasantry in 1764 and 1765, a Chinese house rebuilt by W. J. Müller in the west part of the palace garden in 1783, another built by Müller in the palace kitchen garden in 1780, and two Chinese pavilions adjoining the Erbprinzenstrasse on Margravine Amalie's estate

40.1 DETAILS OF ROOF-HOISTING MECHANISM
Ink and watercolor on wove paper
44.5 × 35 cm
Signed and dated "F inv. & fec/II 1803"

42 ENGRAVINGS FROM THE
TASCHENBUCH FÜR NATUR- UND GARTENFREUNDE
This short-lived journal served the interest in English-style landscape gardening that flourished in Germany around 1800; the illustrated buildings, however, are French in character, designed by Stuttgart architect Nikolaus Friedrich Thouret and engraved by Christian Friedrich Duttenhofer, both friends of Weinbrenner; the six plates are attached to three album pages

42.1 SMALL COUNTRY HOUSE: PLAN AND ELEVATION
Mixed engraving and etching on wove paper
13 × 13.5 cm
c. 1800
Marked "N. T[h]ouret inv." and "Duttenhofer sc."

42.2 GARDEN HOUSE: ELEVATION
Mixed engraving and etching on wove paper
7.5 × 12.5 cm
c. 1800

42.3 FOUNTAIN: PLAN, TWO ELEVATIONS, AND SECTION
Mixed engraving and etching on wove paper
13.5 × 12.5 cm
Marked "N. Thouret 1799"

42.4 SPORTS PAVILION: ELEVATION
Mixed engraving and etching on wove paper
7.5 × 13 cm
c. 1800

42.5 GARDEN HOUSE: PLAN AND ELEVATION
Mixed engraving and etching on wove paper
11 × 13 cm
c. 1800
Marked "Thouret inv." and "Duttenhofer sc."

42.6 GARDEN HOUSE: PLAN
Mixed engraving and etching on wove paper
8.5 × 12.5 cm
c. 1800

44 WEINBRENNER HOUSE, KARLSRUHE
Friedrich Weinbrenner, architect
See cats. 35, 36 for project description

*44.1 GROUND PLAN AND FRONT ELEVATION (cat. 35)
Ink and watercolor on laid paper

32.5 × 50 cm
c. 1801

*44.2 FIRST FLOOR ABOVE GROUND PLAN
AND REAR ELEVATION (cat. 36)
Ink, graphite, and watercolor on laid paper
32 × 49.5 cm
c. 1801

46 SCHNABEL HOUSE, KARLSRUHE
Friedrich Weinbrenner, architect
Built in 1815–16 on the Lange Strasse east of
the Garnisonkirche as a speculative apartment
building for an accountant

46.1 GROUND, FIRST, AND SECOND
FLOOR ABOVE GROUND PLANS
Ink, graphite, and wash on laid paper
41.5 × 47.5 cm
Signed "Thierry" and dated "29 Aug. 1822"

48 NORTHEAST RONDELLPLATZ (BECK,
JÖSLIN, AND REUTLINGER HOUSES),
KARLSRUHE
Friedrich Weinbrenner, architect
See cat. 37 for project description

*48.1 GROUND PLAN (cat. 37)
Ink, graphite, and watercolor on laid paper
50.5 × 64.5 cm
After 1809

48.2 FIRST FLOOR ABOVE GROUND PLAN
Ink, graphite, and watercolor on laid paper
50.5 × 62.5 cm
After 1809

50 LESEGESELLSCHAFT (FORMER BECK
HOUSE), KARLSRUHE
Alterations for the Beck house after its acquisi-
tion by the Lesegesellschaft in 1830

50.1 GROUND AND FIRST FLOOR ABOVE
GROUND PLANS
Ink, graphite, and watercolor on laid paper

22 × 44 cm
c. 1830

52 KUSEL HOUSES, KARLSRUHE
Friedrich Weinbrenner, architect
See cat. 44 for project description

*52.1 GROUND, MEZZANINE, FIRST, AND
SECOND FLOOR ABOVE GROUND
PLANS AND FRONT ELEVATION
(cat. 44)
Ink, graphite, and watercolor on laid paper
57.5 × 45 cm
c. 1812

54 REINHARD HOUSE, KARLSRUHE
Friedrich Weinbrenner, architect
House on the Steinstrasse for a prominent
businessman; signature apparently is that of
contractor Christoph Holb

54.1 REAR ELEVATION
Ink, graphite, and watercolor on laid paper
27 × 42 cm
c. 1812

54.2 GROUND AND FIRST FLOOR ABOVE
GROUND PLANS
Ink, graphite, and wash on wove paper
37 × 30 cm
c. 1812
Signed "Holb"

56 HOLB HOUSE, KARLSRUHE
Friedrich Weinbrenner, architect
See cats. 41–43 for project description

*56.1 VERSION 2: GROUND AND FIRST
FLOOR ABOVE GROUND PLANS,
FRONT AND REAR ELEVATIONS
(cat. 43)
Ink, graphite, and watercolor on laid paper
49 × 33.5 cm
c. 1815

*56.2 VERSION 1: FRONT ELEVATION
(cat. 41)
Ink, graphite, and watercolor on laid paper
32.5 × 28.5 cm
1815
Signed "Holb"

*56.3 VERSION 1: SECTION *(cat. 42)*
Ink, graphite, and watercolor on laid paper
31 × 46.5 cm
1815

56.4 VERSION 1: SECOND FLOOR ABOVE
GROUND PLAN
Ink, graphite, and watercolor on laid paper
48.5 × 31 cm
1815

56.5 VERSION 1: GROUND PLAN
Ink, graphite, and wash on laid paper
45.5 × 28.5 cm
1815

58 FICHTBAUER HOUSE
Karl Thierry, architect
Confectioner's establishment, including a shop,
storerooms, six kitchens, and a public dining
room *(see 60.1)*

58.1 LONG ELEVATION
Ink, graphite, and watercolor on wove paper
32.5 × 17.5 cm
c. 1817

58.2 SHORT ELEVATION
Ink, graphite, and watercolor on wove paper
32.5 × 17.5 cm
Signed and dated "gez. von Carl
Thierry,/im Mon. Marz. 1817"

58.3 SECTION
Ink, graphite, and watercolor on wove paper
32.5 × 17.5 cm
Signed "gez. v. C. Thierry/im Mon. Marz."

58.4 GROUND PLAN
Ink, graphite, and wash on wove paper
32.5 × 17.5 cm
Signed and dated "gez. v. Carl Thierry/im
Mon. Marz. 1817"

58.5 FIRST FLOOR ABOVE GROUND PLAN
Ink, graphite, and wash on wove paper
32.5 × 17.5 cm
Signed and dated "gez. von Carl Thierry/im
Mon. Marz 1817"

58.6 SECOND FLOOR ABOVE GROUND
PLAN
Ink, graphite, and wash on wove paper
32.5 × 17.5 cm
Signed and dated "gez v. C. Thierry/im
Mon. Marz 1817"

60 SPITALTOR PLAN (CITY UNIDENTIFIED)
Plan of the area around the Spitaltor, showing
the site of the Fichtbauer house (58.1–58.6);
adjacent streets are labeled Steinweg,
Webergasse, Spitalgasse, and Jungfernsteig

60.1 PLAN
Ink, graphite, and watercolor on wove paper
33 × 39.5 cm
Signed and dated "gez. von Carl Thierry/im
Mon. Feb. 1817"

62 HERTZER HOUSE, BADEN-BADEN
Friedrich Weinbrenner, architect
See cats. 45, 46 for project description

*62.1 GROUND AND FIRST FLOOR ABOVE
GROUND PLANS AND SIDE
ELEVATION *(cat. 45)*
Ink, graphite, and watercolor on wove paper
46 × 31 cm
Signed and dated "Thierry 1824"

*62.2 FRONT ELEVATION AND SECTION
(cat. 46)
Ink, graphite, and watercolor on wove paper

33.5 × 26.5 cm
c. 1824

64 INN, KARLSRUHE (?)
School of Weinbrenner
Corner tavern with four barrooms

   64.1 GROUND AND FIRST FLOOR ABOVE
       GROUND PLANS
       Ink, graphite, and watercolor on wove paper
       28.5 × 42 cm

66 TRIANGULAR HOUSE *A*,
   KARLSRUHE (?)
Peculiar scheme for either a corner house or a
house diagonally partitioned, possibly a student exercise

   66.1 GROUND AND UPPER FLOOR PLANS
       (recto) SECTION AND ELEVATION OF
       BALUSTRADE (verso)
       Ink and graphite on laid paper
       24.5 × 37 cm

68 TRIANGULAR HOUSE *B*,
   KARLSRUHE (?)
Another scheme for a triangular house, with
some continuity implied in the adjoining site

   68.1 BASEMENT, GROUND, AND FIRST
       FLOOR ABOVE GROUND PLANS AND
       FRONT ELEVATION
       Ink, graphite, and wash on laid paper
       48 × 11.5 cm

70 CHRISTOPH ARNOLD HOUSE,
   KARLSRUHE
Christoph Arnold, architect
Arnold's house, built in 1806, displays a typical
resolution of the difficulties of its corner site
between the Wald- and Erbprinzenstrassen on

the Ludwigsplatz, with a diagonal stair and
rooms arranged to either side

   70.1 GROUND PLAN
       Ink and graphite on wove paper
       51 × 31 cm

72 INN WITH POST OFFICE,
   KARLSRUHE (?)
Awkward and crudely drawn design for a cor-
ner site

   72.1 GROUND AND FIRST FLOOR ABOVE
       GROUND PLANS AND ELEVATION
       Ink and graphite on laid paper
       43.5 × 67.5 cm

74 CORNER HOUSE, KARLSRUHE
Friedrich Arnold, architect (?)
See cat. 39 for project description

   *74.1 GROUND PLAN AND SIDE
       ELEVATION *(cat. 39)*
       Ink, graphite, and watercolor on wove paper
       30.5 × 46 cm
       Signed "C. Eichelkraut"

76 77 ZÄHRINGERSTRASSE, KARLSRUHE
Ferdinand (?) Thierry, architect
Design for an awkward site on the west end of
the rapidly developing Zähringerstrasse, altered only slightly in execution

   76.1 GROUND PLAN
       Ink, graphite, and wash on laid paper
       47.5 × 31 cm
       Marked "gebaut entworfen von/Thierry"

78 ATTACHED HOUSE, KARLSRUHE (?)
School of Weinbrenner
See cat. 40 for project description

*78.1 SECOND FLOOR ABOVE GROUND
PLAN AND FRONT ELEVATION (cat. 40)
Ink, graphite, and watercolor on wove paper
52.5 × 31 cm

80 SOUTHWEST RONDELLPLATZ,
KARLSRUHE
Christoph Arnold, architect (?)
Plans for two houses adjacent to the Stemmer-
man house (1809), all apparently by Christoph
Arnold

80.1 GROUND AND FIRST FLOOR ABOVE
GROUND PLANS
Ink, graphite, and watercolor on laid paper
57.5 × 48 cm

82 PAINTER'S HOUSE, KARLSRUHE (?)
Friedrich Weinbrenner, architect
See cat. 38 for project description

*82.1 GROUND AND FIRST FLOOR ABOVE
GROUND PLANS, FRONT AND SIDE
ELEVATIONS AND SECTION (cat. 38)
Ink, graphite, and wash on laid paper
66 × 48.5 cm
c. 1800

84 COUNTRY HOUSE FOR THE KING OF
WÜRTTEMBERG
Friedrich Weinbrenner, architect
Basement of this immense Palladian villa is divided by a passageway through which carriages
could travel under the building and where pas-
sengers could alight; design anticipates Weinbrenner's Palladian villa of 1817 for Christiane
Louise (see cats. 1–3)

84.1 PLAN OF BASEMENT
Ink and wash on tracing paper
30 × 49 cm
c. 1806

86 SUMMER PALACE FOR QUEEN
FRIEDERIKE OF SWEDEN (?),
BADEN-BADEN
Friedrich Weinbrenner, architect
See cat. 22 for project description

*86.1 GROUND PLAN AND FRONT, REAR,
AND SIDE ELEVATIONS (cat. 22)
Ink, graphite, watercolor, and wash on laid
paper
47 × 52 cm
c. 1820

88 COUNTRY HOUSE, AARAU
Friedrich Weinbrenner, architect
See cats. 23, 24 for project description

*88.1 FRONT AND REAR ELEVATIONS,
GROUND PLAN, AND FIRST FLOOR
ABOVE GROUND PLAN (cat. 23)
Ink, watercolor, and wash on laid paper
40.5 × 61 cm

*88.2 SIDE ELEVATION AND TRANSVERSE
SECTION (cat. 24)
Ink, graphite, watercolor, and wash on laid
paper
30 × 50 cm

90 PALLADIAN HOUSE
School of Weinbrenner
Wooden, Palladian country house with pedimented, one-room, central block flanked by
wings and with entrance stairs leading to a
deep porch screened by a baseless Doric order

90.1 FRONT ELEVATION
Ink, graphite, watercolor, and wash on laid
paper
25 × 49.5 cm

90.2 SIDE ELEVATION
Ink, graphite, watercolor, and wash on laid
paper
31.5 × 42.5 cm

90.3 REAR ELEVATION
Ink, graphite, watercolor, and wash on laid
    paper
25 × 49.5 cm

90.4 GROUND PLAN
Ink, graphite, watercolor, and wash on laid
    paper
31.5 × 49.5 cm

92 HALF-TIMBERED COUNTRY HOUSE
Ferdinand (?) Thierry, architect
See cats. 25–27 for project description

*92.1 NORTH ELEVATION *(cat. 26)*
Ink, watercolor, and wash on laid paper
24 × 52 cm
c. 1830
Signed "Thierry f."

*92.2 EAST ELEVATION *(cat. 27)*
Ink, watercolor, and wash on laid paper
24 × 52 cm
c. 1830
Signed "Thierry f."

*92.3 NORTH, WEST, AND EAST
ELEVATIONS AND GROUND PLAN
(cat. 25)
Ink, watercolor, and wash on laid paper
53 × 73.5 cm
c. 1830
Drawn by Ferdinand Thierry (?)

94 PALACE FOR GRAND DUKE KARL AND
GRAND DUCHESS STEPHANIE,
BADENWEILER
Friedrich Arnold, architect
Ideal project for the grand duke and duchess of
Baden, designed in 1812; large C-shaped plan
organized around central rooms with screened
apses on each floor

94.1 GROUND PLAN
Ink and wash on wove paper

31 × 44 cm
c. 1812
Signed "Fr. Arnold"

94.2 FIRST FLOOR ABOVE GROUND PLAN
Ink and wash on wove paper
31 × 44 cm
c. 1812
Signed "Fr. Arnold"

96 CASTLE NEU-EBERSTEIN
Friedrich Weinbrenner, architect
Thirteenth-century castle near Gernsbach re-
built by Weinbrenner in 1803–4 for Margrave
Friedrich, the second son of Karl Friedrich, the
elector of Baden; these drawings may have been
intended for publication in Weinbrenner's
Gebäude (1822–35)

96.1 FIRST FLOOR ABOVE GROUND PLAN
AND REAR ELEVATION
Ink, graphite, and wash on laid paper
40.5 × 27 cm
c. 1821 (?)

96.2 GROUND PLAN AND SIDE
ELEVATION
Ink, graphite, and wash on laid paper
40.5 × 26.5 cm
c. 1821 (?)

96.3 TRANSVERSE AND LONGITUDINAL
SECTIONS
Ink and graphite on laid paper
39.5 × 26.5 cm
c. 1821 (?)

98 COUNTRY HOUSE *A*
Karl Thierry, architect (?)
One-and-one-half-story jerkin-head–roofed
farmhouse with pedimented central block

98.1 GROUND PLAN, FIRST FLOOR ABOVE
GROUND PLAN, AND FRONT AND
SIDE ELEVATIONS

Ink and graphite on laid paper
74 × 53 cm
Signed and dated "d. 23tn 3/15/C.
  Th.[ierry] fec."

100 COUNTRY HOUSE *B*
Ferdinand (?) Thierry, architect (?)
Large country house with bathing pool in the
basement and a two-story main hall decorated
by a palmette frieze

100.1 TRANSVERSE SECTION, GROUND
PLAN, FIRST FLOOR ABOVE GROUND
PLAN, AND BASEMENT PLAN
(SUPERIMPOSED ON GROUND PLAN)
Ink, graphite, watercolor, and wash on laid
  paper
49 × 31.5 cm
Signed and dated on verso "Carlsruh 28tn
  May 1812/Thierry"

102 COUNTRY HOUSE *C*
School of Weinbrenner
Compact Palladian house with pedimented
central bay and hip-roofed main block; horse
stalls in wing to left and carriage house to right

102.1 GROUND PLAN, FIRST FLOOR ABOVE
GROUND PLAN, AND FRONT
ELEVATION
Ink, graphite, watercolor, and wash on laid
  paper
50 × 31 cm

104 COUNTRY HOUSE *D*
Michel, architect (?)
Plan for the floor under the roof, divided into
living quarters for farm workers

104.1 TOP FLOOR PLAN
Ink, graphite, watercolor, and wash on wove
  paper
28.5 × 41 cm
Signed "Michel"

106 HUNTING LODGE, RUDOLSTADT
Ferdinand Thierry, architect (?)
Stark design for a house in Rudolstadt, where
both Ferdinand and Wilhelm Thierry worked

106.1 FRONT AND REAR ELEVATIONS
Ink, graphite, and watercolor on laid paper
36.5 × 24.5 cm

108 WOODCUTTER'S HOUSE
Friedrich Weinbrenner, architect
Square house in rectangular walled precinct,
flanked by two pavilions; attributed on the
basis of Schumacher, 15r–16r. 108.2 and 108.3
are perhaps contract drawings, signed by
builder Christoph Holb

108.1 VERSION 1: GROUND PLAN AND
ELEVATION
Ink, graphite, watercolor, and wash on laid
  paper
41 × 26.5 cm

108.2 VERSION 2: GROUND PLAN AND
FRONT ELEVATION
Ink, watercolor, and wash on laid paper
48.5 × 28.5 cm
Initialed "H[olb]" (?)

108.3 VERSION 2: FIRST FLOOR ABOVE
GROUND PLAN AND LONGITUDINAL
SECTION
Ink, watercolor, and wash on laid paper
48.5 × 28.5 cm
Initialed "H[olb]" (?)

110 FARM, KATHARINENTAL
Friedrich Weinbrenner, architect
See cats. 33, 34 for project description

*110.1 GROUND PLAN, EAST ELEVATION OF
HOUSE, AND EAST ELEVATION OF
HAY BARN WITH TRANSVERSE
SECTIONS OF COW SHEDS *(cat. 34)*
Ink, graphite, watercolor, and wash on laid
  paper

53.5 × 45.5 cm
c. 1808–9

*110.2 YARD ELEVATION OF A COW SHED,
WEST ELEVATION OF HOUSE WITH
TRANSVERSE SECTIONS OF COW
SHEDS, AND TRANSVERSE
SECTIONS OF HOUSE AND HAY
BARN (cat. 33)
Ink, graphite, watercolor, and wash on laid
paper
53.5 × 45.5 cm
c. 1808–9

112 FARM, RITTERHECK
Friedrich Weinbrenner, architect
See cat. 32 for project description

*112.1 GROUND PLAN, FRONT ELEVATION
OF COTTAGES AND BARN, SIDE
ELEVATION OF A COTTAGE, AND
TRANSVERSE SECTIONS OF A
COTTAGE AND THE BARN (cat. 32)
Ink, graphite, watercolor, and wash on laid
paper
56 × 45 cm
Marked "von Fr. Weinbrenner" and dated
"d 13 August 1813"

114 FARM (UNIDENTIFIED)
School of Weinbrenner
Rectangular farm complex with more elaborate
house than Ritterheck or Katharinental; sheds
for horses, cows, pigs, and sheep indicated, as
well as large hay barn

114.1 FIRST FLOOR ABOVE GROUND PLAN,
SIDE ELEVATION OF COMPLEX, AND
LONGITUDINAL SECTION OF
COMPLEX
Ink, graphite, watercolor, and wash on laid
paper
46 × 31 cm

114.2 GROUND PLAN, FRONT ELEVATION
OF COMPLEX, AND TRANSVERSE
SECTION OF COMPLEX

Ink, graphite, watercolor, and wash on laid
paper
46 × 31 cm

116 FARMHOUSE, GROFISCH
School of Weinbrenner (Wilhelm Thierry?)
See cat. 28 for project description

*116.1 FRONT ELEVATION, GROUND PLAN,
AND FIRST FLOOR ABOVE GROUND
PLAN (cat. 28)
Ink and graphite on laid paper
52 × 26.5 cm

118 BARN AND HOUSE
School of Weinbrenner
Farmhouse at left, hay barn with ventilation
slits at center, and horse and cow stalls at right

118.1 ELEVATION, GROUND PLAN, AND
FIRST FLOOR ABOVE GROUND PLAN
Ink, graphite, and wash on laid paper
36 × 52.5 cm

120 SHEEP SHED, BAUSCHLOTT
Friedrich Weinbrenner, architect
See cat. 30 for project description

*120.1 FRONT AND SIDE ELEVATIONS,
TRANSVERSE SECTION, AND
GROUND PLAN (cat. 30)
Ink and watercolor on laid paper
51 × 35.5 cm
c. 1805
Initialed "F.W.B." (Weinbrenner?)

120.2 FRONT AND SIDE ELEVATIONS,
TRANSVERSE SECTION, AND
GROUND PLAN
Ink on varnished paper
24 × 25 cm
Later copy of 120.1

122 HALF-TIMBERED BARN
School of Weinbrenner
See cat. 31 for project description

*122.1 ELEVATION, GROUND PLAN, AND
TRANSVERSE SECTION *(cat. 31)*
Ink, graphite, watercolor, and wash on laid
paper
50.5 × 30.5 cm

124 BARN *A*
School of Weinbrenner
Double barn under a jerkin-head roof with
pedimented doors

124.1 GROUND PLAN AND SIDE AND
FRONT ELEVATIONS
Ink and wash on laid paper
31 × 52 cm

126 BARN *B*
School of Weinbrenner
See cat. 29 for project description

*126.1 GROUND PLAN, FRONT ELEVATION,
AND LONGITUDINAL SECTION
(cat. 29)
Ink, watercolor, and wash on laid paper
47.5 × 30.5 cm

128 BARN *C*
School of Weinbrenner
Single-vessel barn with three attached work-
rooms under their own roofs

128.1 GROUND PLAN AND FRONT AND
SIDE ELEVATIONS
Ink, graphite, watercolor, and wash on laid
paper
30.5 × 37 cm

130 BARN *D*
School of Weinbrenner
A quatrefoil dormer window, pilasters, and

louvered windows lend dignity to this ornate
barn, perhaps a dairy

130.1 GROUND PLAN AND FRONT
ELEVATION
Ink, graphite, watercolor, and wash on laid
paper
34 × 20.5 cm
Signed "L. Fugergi" and dated "20/2/1830"

132 BARN *E*
School of Weinbrenner
Large barn with hayloft

132.1 TRANSVERSE SECTION
Ink, graphite, watercolor, and wash on laid
paper
29.5 × 22.5 cm

134 CARRIAGE HOUSE
School of Weinbrenner
Half-timbered, two-bay carriage house; living
quarters on the upper floor heated by a stove

134.1 FRONT ELEVATION AND
TRANSVERSE SECTION
Ink, graphite, watercolor, and wash on laid
paper
45 × 27 cm

136 WASH HOUSE
School of Weinbrenner
Wooden laundry building with washing and
drying rooms

136.1 GROUND PLAN, FIRST FLOOR ABOVE
GROUND PLAN, FRONT AND SIDE
ELEVATION, AND TRANSVERSE
SECTION
Ink on laid paper
33 × 22 cm
Signature torn away

144 RIDING SCHOOL, KARLSRUHE
Friedrich Weinbrenner, architect
See cats. 57, 58 for project description

*144.1 FRONT ELEVATION AND GROUND
PLAN (recto) *(cat. 58)* THE DRINKING
CONTEST BETWEEN HERAKLES
AND DIONYSUS (verso)
Ink, graphite, and wash on laid paper
36 × 25 cm
Watermark "Fabriano"
c. 1795

*144.2 TRANSVERSE SECTION AND SIDE
ELEVATION (recto) *(cat. 57)*
ARCHITECTURAL STUDIES (verso)
Ink, graphite, and wash on laid paper
25 × 36 cm
c. 1795

146 GIRLS' SCHOOL, KARLSRUHE
This school stood on the Ritterstrasse between
the Zähringerstrasse and the *Landgrabe*

146.1 FIRST FLOOR ABOVE GROUND PLAN
Ink, graphite, and wash on laid paper with
overlay
26 × 42.5 cm
Dated "30ten Mai 1826."

146.2 SECOND FLOOR ABOVE GROUND
PLAN
Ink, graphite, and wash on laid paper with
overlay
28 × 42.5 cm
c. 1826

148 MILITARY SCHOOL, KARLSRUHE
Friedrich Arnold, architect
Located on the Hans-Thoma-Strasse, this
building built in 1824–25 has been vastly
altered

148.1 FRONT ELEVATION AND GROUND
PLAN (recto) VON BECK HOUSE SITE
PLAN (verso)
Ink, graphite, and wash on laid paper
25.5 × 45 cm
c. 1824–25

150 POLYTECHNICAL SCHOOL,
KARLSRUHE
Heinrich Hübsch, architect
Final, T-shaped plan for the new school on the
Lange Strasse; these are perhaps contract draw-
ings, signed by the builder Holb

150.1 FIRST FLOOR ABOVE GROUND PLAN
Ink, graphite, and wash on wove paper
32 × 43 cm
c. 1831
Signed "Holb" and marked "von H. Hübsch
erb."

150.2 SECOND FLOOR ABOVE GROUND
PLAN
Ink, graphite, and wash on wove paper
31 × 47 cm
c. 1831
Signed "Holb"

152 ARSENAL, KARLSRUHE
Friedrich Weinbrenner, architect
See cats. 47, 48 for project description

*152.1 LONGITUDINAL SECTION THROUGH
OUTER COURTYARD *(cat. 48)*
Ink and graphite on laid paper
28 × 46.5 cm
c. 1795

*152.2 INNER COURTYARD PERSPECTIVE
(cat. 47)
Ink on wove paper
26.5 × 38 cm

154 POWDER MAGAZINE, KARLSRUHE
Friedrich Weinbrenner, architect
Now demolished; built in 1815 outside Karlsruhe between Bulach and Grünwinkel to
supplement a magazine designed by Weinbrenner in 1806

154.1 GROUND PLAN (recto)
ARCHITECTURE AND NATURE
STUDIES (verso)

Ink, graphite, watercolor, and wash on laid
paper
39.5 × 26.5 cm
Initialed "fArd." and marked "aufgen:
1818/und gezeichnet/durch Cap.
[Friedrich] Arnold"

156 TURKISH BATH, BADEN-BADEN (?)
Friedrich Weinbrenner, architect
See cat. 59 for project description

*156.1 TRANSVERSE SECTION *(cat. 59)*
Ink, graphite, watercolor, and wash on laid
paper
23 × 33.5 cm
Marked "gezeichnet von. F. Weinbrenner"

158 PUBLIC BATHS
Friedrich Weinbrenner, architect (?)
Unidentified project for a public bath complex
consisting of a two-story house, eighteen
bathing cubicles aligned behind colonnades,
and a stable

158.1 FRONT ELEVATION AND GROUND
PLAN
Ink, graphite, watercolor, and wash on laid
paper
47 × 31.5 cm

160 GUARD HOUSE, KARLSRUHE
Friedrich Weinbrenner, architect
See cat. 49 for project description

*160.1 FRONT ELEVATION AND GROUND
PLAN *(cat. 49)*
Ink, graphite, watercolor, and wash on laid
paper
37.5 × 31 cm
c. 1805–6
Signed "Fr. Weinbrenner"

162 GOVERNMENT HOUSE, KARLSRUHE
Christoph and Friedrich Arnold, architects

Located at the Innerer Zirkel and the Adler-
strasse; built in 1812 as a private residence by
Christoph Arnold and remodeled by his
brother Friedrich as quarters for the War Min-
istry in 1818

162.1 FIRST FLOOR ABOVE GROUND PLAN
Ink, graphite, and wash on laid paper
39.5 × 27 cm
Signed "fArd" and marked "aufgen:
1818./ud. gezeichnet/durch Cap: Arnold"
and "erhalt[?], d. 16/3.47."

162.2 SECOND FLOOR ABOVE GROUND
PLAN
Ink, graphite, and wash on laid paper
39 × 26.5 cm
c. 1818

162.3 THIRD FLOOR ABOVE GROUND
PLAN
Ink, graphite, and wash on laid paper
39 × 26.5 cm
c. 1818

162.4 FIRST FLOOR ABOVE GROUND PLAN
Ink, graphite, and wash on laid paper
39.5 × 26 cm
c. 1818

162.5 SECOND FLOOR ABOVE GROUND
PLAN
Ink, graphite, and wash on laid paper
29.5 × 27 cm
c. 1818

162.6 THIRD FLOOR ABOVE GROUND
PLAN
Ink, graphite, and wash on laid paper
39.5 × 26.5 cm
c. 1818

164 THEATER, GOTHA
Friedrich Weinbrenner, architect
See cat. 51 for project description

*164.1 GROUND PLAN AND FRONT, REAR,
AND SIDE ELEVATIONS (recto) *(cat. 51)*

ARCHITECTURE, FIGURE, AND
HANDWRITING STUDIES (verso)
Ink, graphite, color pencil, watercolor, and
  wash on laid paper
53 × 37 cm
c. 1812

166 SYNAGOGUE, KARLSRUHE
Friedrich Weinbrenner, architect
See cat. 50 for project description

*166.1 FRONT ELEVATION *(cat. 50)*
Ink, graphite, watercolor, and wash on laid
  paper
35.5 × 51 cm
1798

168 CARL FRIEDRICH, LEOPOLD, AND SOPHIE FOUNDATION, KARLSRUHE
Friedrich Fischer, architect
City's first almshouse, built 1831–33; now
destroyed

168.1 GROUND PLAN, FIRST FLOOR ABOVE
GROUND PLAN, AND FRONT
ELEVATION
Lithograph on wove paper
39 × 28 cm
Marked "Fr. Fischer inv." and "Lith. von P.
  Wagner in Carlsruhe"

170 PUBLIC HALL, KARLSRUHE OR BADEN-BADEN (?)
Friedrich Weinbrenner or Ferdinand Thierry,
architect
Unidentified design for a public hall with por-
ticos at both ends, perhaps related to Weinbrenner's "Promenadenhaus" project for
Baden-Baden of 1802

170.1 GROUND PLAN
Ink, graphite, and wash on wove (carton)
  paper
26 × 21 cm
Signed "Ferd. Thierry"

172 CEMETERY GATE, KARLSRUHE
Friedrich Weinbrenner, architect (?)
See cat. 52 for project description

*172.1 GROUND PLAN, FRONT AND REAR
ELEVATIONS, AND TRANSVERSE
SECTION *(cat. 52)*
Ink, graphite, watercolor, and wash on wove
  paper
43.5 × 30 cm
c. 1803–4 (?)

174 MORTUARY, KARLSRUHE
Friedrich Weinbrenner, architect (?)
See cat. 54 for project description

*174.1 SIDE ELEVATION AND GROUND
PLAN *(cat. 54)*
Ink, graphite, watercolor, and wash on laid
  paper
46 × 31.5 cm
c. 1812 (?)

176 CEMETERY HALL, KARLSRUHE
Friedrich Weinbrenner or August Mossbrug-
ger, architect (?)
See cat. 53 for project description

*176.1 LONGITUDINAL AND TRANSVERSE
SECTIONS *(cat. 53)*
Ink, graphite, watercolor, and wash on laid
  paper
30.5 × 46 cm
Signed and dated "[August] Mossbrugger
  fec/im Jan 1825."

178 FRAU SCHMIDTBAUER MONUMENT, KARLSRUHE
Karl Thierry, architect
Wall monument designed for a female member
of the prominent Schmidtbauer family

178.1 ELEVATIONS AND DETAILS
Graphite on laid paper

34.5 × 21.5 cm
Marked "ausgeführt 1841 durch C. Thierry"

180 VICTORY MONUMENT, LEIPZIG
Friedrich Weinbrenner, architect
See cat. 55 for project description

*180.1 SITE PLAN AND ELEVATION OF ONE
PAVILION *(cat. 55)*
Ink, watercolor, and wash on laid paper
33 × 47.5 cm
1814 or later

182 RADIAL-PLAN PUBLIC MONUMENT
Friedrich Weinbrenner, architect (?)
Large, central-plan pedestal, probably for a
war memorial or national monument

182.1 PLAN (recto)
VAULTED INTERIOR PERSPECTIVE
(verso)
Ink and graphite on laid paper
20 × 27.5 cm

184 COLUMN PEDESTALS AND HEATING
STOVES
Friedrich Weinbrenner, architect (?)
Two column pedestals for the interior of an
unidentified hall with heating units indicated

184.1 ELEVATIONS
Ink and graphite on laid paper
16 × 21 cm
Dated "d 28ten Marz 1815"

186 PUBLIC FOUNTAINS, KARLSRUHE
Friedrich Weinbrenner, architect
Studies for three wall fountains, possibly for
Margravine Christiane Louise's estate

186.1 ELEVATIONS AND PLAN
Graphite on laid paper
34 × 21 cm
c. 1817

188 PUBLIC FOUNTAINS, KARLSRUHE
Friedrich Weinbrenner, architect
Five fountains, perhaps designed in connection
with the enlargement of the city

188.1 ELEVATIONS AND PLAN
Ink on laid paper
22 × 23 cm
c. 1809–15.

190 FOUNTAIN, ANSPACH
Friedrich Weinbrenner, architect (?)
Project for a cast iron public fountain with a
statue of a knight, in Anspach, about 10 km
northwest of Frankfurt

190.1 ELEVATION AND FIGURE STUDY
Graphite on wove paper
23 × 18 cm

192 GOTHIC PUBLIC MONUMENTS AND
OBELISK, KARLSRUHE
Possibly a student drawing that shows four
fountain and monument projects designed for
the growing city

192.1 ELEVATIONS AND PLANS
Graphite on laid paper
21 × 13.5 cm
Dated "d. 10'Oct. 40" and "d 13 Oct."

194 *ARCHITEKTONISCHES LEHRBUCH*
Friedrich Weinbrenner, author
See cats. 56, 73–79 for project description

194.1 ROTATIONS OF SOLID FIGURES
(Vol. 1, fasc. 1, pl. 4)
Engraving on wove paper
22 × 28 cm
1810

194.2 LANDSCAPED PARK IN PERSPECTIVE
(Vol. 2, fasc. 1, pl. 1)
Engraving with graphite emendations on
wove paper

30 × 46 cm
1817 (?)

194.3 LANDSCAPED PARK IN PERSPECTIVE
(Preparatory drawing for vol. 2, fasc. 3,
pl. 10)
Ink on laid paper
36 × 23.5 cm
c. 1824

*194.4 FORESHORTENED PLANE FIGURES
(cat. 78)
(Preparatory drawing for vol. 2, fasc. 3,
pl. 12)
Ink and wash on laid paper
22 × 31.5 cm
c. 1824
Signed "fArd. Arnold"

194.5 FORESHORTENED PLANE FIGURES
(Preparatory drawing for vol. 2, fasc. 3,
pl. 12)
Ink and wash on laid paper
22 × 30.5 cm
c. 1824
Signed "fArd. Arnold"

194.6 CAST SHADOW STUDIES
(Vol. 2, fasc. 4, pl. 18)
Engraving on wove paper
21.5 × 30 cm
1824

*194.7 DORIC ENTABLATURE IN
PERSPECTIVE (cat. 79)
(Preparatory drawing for vol. 2, fasc. 5,
pl. 30)
Ink and graphite on wove paper
27 × 41 cm
c. 1824

*194.8 PERSPECTIVE VIEW UP STAIRS (cat. 75)
(Rendered study for vol. 2, fasc. 6, pl. 31)
Ink, graphite, and wash on laid paper
37 × 52 cm
c. 1824

*194.9 PERSPECTIVE VIEW UP STAIRS (cat. 77)
(Vol. 2, fasc. 6, pl. 31)

Lithograph on wove paper
33 × 47 cm
1824

*194.10 PERSPECTIVE VIEW UP STAIRS (cat. 76)
(Preparatory drawing for vol. 2, fasc. 6,
pl. 31)
Ink and graphite on laid paper
27 × 39.5 cm
c. 1824

*194.11 PERSPECTIVE VIEW DOWN STAIRS
(cat. 74)
(Rendered study for vol. 2, fasc. 6, pl. 32)
Ink, graphite, and wash on laid paper
35.5 × 51 cm
c. 1824

*194.12 PERSPECTIVE VIEW DOWN STAIRS
(cat. 73)
(Rendered study for vol. 2, fasc. 6, pl. 32)
Ink, graphite, and wash on laid paper
36 × 52.5 cm
c. 1824

194.13 PERSPECTIVE OF RATHAUS
VESTIBULE
(Vol. 2, fasc. 6, pl. 36)
Lithograph on laid paper
33 × 47.5 cm
1824
Printed initials "C. T[hierry?]."

194.14 PERSPECTIVE OF MUSEUM
VESTIBULE
(Vol. 2, fasc. 6, pl. 37)
Lithograph on wove paper
28 × 43.5 cm
1824

*194.15 PERSPECTIVE OF BELLE ALLIANCE
MEMORIAL (cat. 56)
(Preparatory drawing for vol. 2, fasc. 6,
pl. 40)
Ink and graphite on laid paper
29.5 × 48 cm
c. 1824

196 STUDIES OF SPEYER CATHEDRAL
School of Weinbrenner
See cats. 81, 82 for project description

*196.1 RESTORED FACADE AND VARIOUS
DETAILS (recto) *(cat. 81)*
VARIOUS ELEVATIONS (verso)
Graphite on wove paper
25 × 38 cm
Probably 1826

*196.2 SCULPTURAL DETAILS *(cat. 82)*
Graphite on wove paper
26.5 × 21 cm
Dated "18 Marz 1826"

198 STUDIES OF ROMANESQUE
ARCHITECTURE
School of Weinbrenner
See cat. 83 for project description

*198.1 ROMANESQUE ARCH FORMS *(cat. 83)*
Graphite on wove paper
19 × 13.5 cm
c. 1826 (?)

198.2 UNIDENTIFIED MEDIEVAL GABLE,
VARIOUS ARCH FORMS
Ink on yellow tracing paper
14 × 21.5 cm
c. 1826 (?)

198.3 WINDOWS FROM SPEYER, GOSLAR,
AND OTHER CATHEDRALS (recto)
VARIOUS GROUPED ROMANESQUE
WINDOWS (verso)
Graphite on wove paper, ruled on verso
21.5 × 17.5 cm
c. 1826 (?)

198.4 VARIOUS ROMANESQUE DETAILS
Graphite on laid paper
21.5 × 18 cm
c. 1826 (?)

198.5 VARIOUS ROMANESQUE DETAILS
Ink and graphite on laid paper

34.5 × 22 cm
c. 1826 (?)

198.6 INCOMPLETE PERSPECTIVE STUDY
(recto)
COVER SHEET FOR
"BYZANTINISCH" DETAILS (verso)
Graphite on wove paper
45 × 38.5 cm
c. 1826 (?)

200 PALLADIAN ARCHITECTURE
Friedrich Weinbrenner or pupil
See cat. 80 for project description

*200.1 DETAILS AND ELEVATIONS OF
PALLADIAN BUILDINGS *(cat. 80)*
Ink and graphite on laid paper
74 × 53 cm
1820s (?)

202 ITALIAN TRAVEL SKETCH
Friedrich Weinbrenner or pupil

202.1 DETAILS OF FOUNTAIN AT VITERBO
Graphite on wove paper
44.5 × 29 cm
1820s (?)

204 GOTHIC ALTAR
Friedrich Weinbrenner (?)

204.1 STUDY
Ink and graphite on laid paper
21.5 × 17 cm
1820s (?)

206 PARISIAN (?) TRAVEL SKETCHES
Friedrich Gilly (?)
See cat. 84 for project description

*206.1 FOUR MEDIEVAL STAGE SETS (?) (recto)
(cat. 84) NEOCLASSICAL INTERIOR
(verso)

Ink, graphite, and wash on laid paper
31.5 × 44 cm
c. 1797

208 ROOFING
School of Weinbrenner

208.1 STUDIES
Graphite on laid paper
34 × 21.5 cm
Inscribed "Kunstverein" and "1831"

210 CEILING DESIGNS
School of Weinbrenner
Studies for panels, probably for the Grand
Ducal Palace, Karlsruhe.
See cats. 60–67 for project description

210.1 PANEL WITH VINE ORNAMENT
Ink and graphite on laid paper
21.5 × 34 cm

210.2 ZODIAC SIGNS
Graphite on laid paper
34.5 × 21.5 cm

210.3 STUDIES FOR PANELS WITH
CIRCULAR BOSSES
Graphite on laid paper
28.5 × 34 cm

210.4 PANEL WITH FLOWER AND VINE
ORNAMENT
Graphite on laid paper
21 × 34.5 cm

210.5 PANEL WITH VINE SCROLL
Ink and graphite on laid paper
20.5 × 29 cm

210.6 BOSS WITH VINE PATTERN
Graphite on laid paper
20.5 × 17.5 cm

210.7 RECTANGULAR PANEL
Graphite on tissue
28.5 × 27 cm

210.8 ROSETTE BOSS
Ink and graphite on laid paper
10 × 19 cm

210.9 BOSS WITH GARNITURE OF
ANCIENT VESSELS
Graphite on laid paper
19 × 24.5 cm

210.10 PANEL WITH VINE PATTERN
Graphite on wove paper
26 × 34 cm

210.11 PANEL WITH VINE PATTERN
Ink and graphite on laid paper
34.5 × 41.5 cm

210.12 ROSETTE BOSS
Graphite on laid paper
34.5 × 41.5 cm

210.13 STUDIES FOR SQUARE PANELS
Graphite on wove paper
26 × 42.5 cm

*210.14 PANEL WITH SWANS *(cat. 68)*
Graphite on laid paper
17 × 20.5 cm

210.15 PANEL WITH VINE PATTERN
Graphite on wove paper
10.5 × 21 cm

210.16 DIAMOND-SHAPED PANELS AND
FLOREATE BOSS
Graphite on wove paper
11.5 × 25.5 cm

210.17 DIAMOND-SHAPED PANEL WITH
VINE SCROLL
Graphite on wove paper
22 × 35 cm

210.18 STUDIES FOR PANELS WITH
GEOMETRIC PATTERNS
Graphite on laid paper
22 × 21 cm

210.19 STUDY FOR GEOMETRIC PANEL
Ink and graphite on laid paper
34.5 × 21 cm

210.20 PANEL WITH SPROUTING VINE
Ink and graphite on wove paper
21.5 × 17.5 cm

210.21 PANEL WITH VINE PATTERN
Graphite on laid paper
22.5 × 34.5 cm

210.22 PANEL WITH ROSETTE BOSS
Graphite on laid paper
19.5 × 24.5 cm

210.23 CEILING IN SIX SECTIONS WITH
SWAN MOTIF
Graphite on laid paper
20 × 33 cm

210.24 PANEL WITH FLOREATE BOSS
Graphite on laid paper
17.5 × 21.5 cm

210.25 PANEL WITH BOSS IN THE FORM OF
A SHIELD
Ink and graphite on laid paper
17 × 22 cm

210.26 PANEL WITH SPROUTING VINE
Ink and graphite on laid paper
21.5 × 18 cm

210.27 PANEL WITH LYRE MOTIF
Graphite on laid paper
23.5 × 13.5 cm

210.28 PANEL WITH TWO BOSS STUDIES
Ink and graphite on laid paper
25.5 × 34 cm

210.29 PANEL WITH VINE AND VASE MOTIF
Graphite on laid paper
49.5 × 72.5 cm

212 CLASSICAL FIGURE
School of Weinbrenner
Seated woman in classical drapery

212.1 PROFILE
Ink on laid paper
21.5 × 8 cm

214 DOME STUDIES
School of Weinbrenner

214.1 TRANSVERSE SECTION
Ink and graphite on laid paper
21 × 17.5 cm

214.2 ELEVATION
Graphite on laid paper
20.5 × 34.5 cm

216 GOBLETS
School of Weinbrenner

216.1 STUDIES FOR THREE GOBLETS WITH
STEPPED FEET
Ink and graphite on laid paper
17 × 20 cm

218 GRAND DUCAL PALACE, KARLSRUHE
Friedrich Weinbrenner, architect
Only securely identified drawings are cited
here
See cats. 60–67 for project description
Related material: 210.1–210.29, 226.1–226.20,
242.1–242.10

218.1 CEILING DECORATION WITH
ROSETTE AND FLOREATE BOSS
Ink and graphite on laid paper
17 × 20 cm

218.2 COLOR STUDIES FOR THE PRIVATE
ROOMS OF THE GRAND DUKE AND
GRAND DUCHESS
Ink and watercolor on laid paper
24.5 × 24.5 cm

*218.3 BED CANOPY *(cat. 67)*
Ink and graphite on laid paper
34 × 21 cm

*218.4 WALL ELEVATION OF BEDROOM
(cat. 61)
Ink and graphite on laid paper
16.5 × 17.5 cm

*218.5 WALL ELEVATION OF MUSIC ROOM
(cat. 62)
Ink and graphite on laid paper
14 × 17 cm

*218.6 WALL ELEVATION OF THE LIVING
ROOMS OF THE GRAND DUKE AND
GRAND DUCHESS (cat. 63)
Ink and graphite on laid paper
15 × 20 cm

*218.7 WALL ELEVATION OF THE LIVING
ROOM OF THE GRAND DUKE (cat. 64)
Ink and graphite on laid paper
16.5 × 19.5 cm

*218.8 MOLDINGS FOR THE GRAND
DUCHESS'S RECEPTION ROOM AND
A BEDROOM (cat. 65)
Ink, graphite, and watercolor on laid paper
28 × 36.5 cm

*218.9 GRIFFIN FRIEZE FOR THE GRAND
DUKE'S ROOM (cat. 66)
Ink, graphite, and watercolor on laid paper
33.5 × 61 cm

218.10 CLOUD AND STAR DECORATION
FOR BEDROOM
Watercolor on laid paper
34 × 41 cm

*218.11 GROUND PLAN FOR THE
APARTMENTS OF GRAND DUCHESS
STEPHANIE (cat. 60)
Graphite on laid paper
64 × 79 cm

220 GRIFFINS
School of Weinbrenner
Renderings of the mythological beast that
figured in the coat of arms of Baden

220.1 GRIFFIN FOR GALLERY DIRECTOR
BECKER
Watercolor on laid paper
34 × 46.5 cm

220.2 STUDY FOR RAMPANT AND SEATED
GRIFFINS
Graphite and watercolor on laid paper
21.5 × 24.5 cm

221 HERM
School of Weinbrenner
Herm stands between Doric columns with
landscape details in the background

221.1 ELEVATION
Watercolor on wove paper
11.5 × 8 cm

223 KATHOLISCHE STADTKIRCHE,
KARLSRUHE
School of Weinbrenner
See cat. 70 for project description

*223.1 DETAIL OF DOME DECORATION
(cat. 70)
Graphite on wove paper
36.5 × 19 cm
Dated "gez. 1823"

224 LIVING ROOM OF THE PRINCESS OF
ORANIEN, BADEN-BADEN (?)
See cat. 72 for project description

*224.1 INTERIOR PERSPECTIVE (cat. 72)
Graphite on wove paper
27 × 42 cm

226 ORNAMENTAL DETAILS
School of Weinbrenner
Many of these were probably prepared for the
Grand Ducal Palace, Karlsruhe
See cats. 60–67 for project description

226.1 FIGURE AND PATTERN STUDY
Graphite on wove paper
33.5 × 21 cm

226.2 LIST OF DECORATIVE MOTIFS
Graphite on laid paper
34 × 21 cm

226.3 COLUMN BASE AND FIGURE STUDY
Graphite on laid paper
10 × 17.5 cm

226.4 ROSETTE PATTERNS
Graphite on wove paper
25.5 × 41.5 cm

226.5 STUDY OF MOLDINGS WITH VINE
PATTERNS
Graphite on laid paper
34 × 20.5 cm

226.6 OBELISK WITH URN
Watercolor on wove paper
11.5 × 11 cm

226.7 REPEAT PATTERN AND MEANDER
Graphite on laid paper
12.5 × 23.5 cm

226.8 PALMETTE
Ink and watercolor on laid paper
20 × 17 cm

226.9 FLOWER AND VINE PATTERN
Graphite on laid paper
12.5 × 10 cm

226.10 VINE PATTERN
Graphite and chalk on yellow tracing paper
15 × 3.5 cm

226.11 GOTHICIZING MEDALLIONS
Graphite on wove paper
20.5 × 26 cm

226.12 LEAF, DART, AND WAVE MOLDING
Graphite on wove paper
21.5 × 27 cm

226.13 FIGURE STUDIES OR TROPHIES
Graphite on wove paper
23.5 × 34.5 cm

226.14 MEANDER PATTERNS
Graphite on laid paper
21 × 21 cm

226.15 MEANDER PATTERNS
Graphite on laid paper
14.5 × 21.5 cm

226.16 MEANDER PATTERNS
Graphite on laid paper
35.5 × 21.5 cm

226.17 PETAL IN STAR PATTERN
Graphite and watercolor on laid paper
21 × 21.5 cm

226.18 LEAF MOLDING
Graphite and watercolor on laid paper
21 × 16 cm

226.19 LEAF AND DART MOLDING WITH
CORNICE PROFILE
Graphite and watercolor on laid paper
28 × 36.5 cm

226.20 EGG AND DART MOLDING
Graphite on laid paper
34 × 20.5 cm

228 PRINTER'S TAILPIECE
Hand-colored engraving, taken from a book

228.1 MASK AND LYRE
Engraving with watercolor on wove paper
7.5 × 11.5 cm

230 STAIRCASE
School of Weinbrenner

230.1 TRANSVERSE SECTION
Graphite on laid paper
12.5 × 35 cm

232 STRASSBURG THEATER
School of Weinbrenner

Drawing depicts Apollo standing on a vine
supported by swans

    232.1 CEILING DETAIL
       Ink and graphite on laid paper
       18.5 × 11 cm

234 TEAPOT
   School of Weinbrenner
   See cat. 71 for project description

    *234.1 SIDE AND HALF FRONT ELEVATION
       (cat. 71)
       Ink, graphite, and watercolor on laid paper
       30 × 40 cm
       Marked "gefertiget d. 25ten August 1813."

236 STENCIL
   See cat. 69 for project description

    *236.1 STENCIL FOR PALMETTE *(cat. 69)*
       Wove paper
       11 × 32.5 cm

238 UNIDENTIFIED THEATER
   School of Weinbrenner
   Large theater with horseshoe-plan auditorium,
   with sketches of goblets and urns

    238.1 SKETCH PLAN
       Ink and graphite on laid paper
       17.5 × 20.5 cm

240 UNIDENTIFIED BUILDING
   Residential (?)

    240.1 PLAN OF THREE ROOMS
       Ink and graphite on laid paper
       20.5 × 39 cm

242 WALL DESIGNS
   School of Weinbrenner
   Many of these were probably prepared for the

Grand Ducal Palace, Karlsruhe
See cats. 60–67 for project description

    242.1 DRAPERY STUDY WITH COLUMNS
       Ink and graphite on laid paper
       21.5 × 11 cm

    242.2 SPANDREL WITH SPROUTING VINE
       Graphite on laid paper
       19 × 14 cm

    242.3 INTERIOR ELEVATION
       Graphite on laid paper
       20.5 × 34.5 cm

    242.4 LUNETTE WITH TWO SCONCES
       Graphite on laid paper
       17 × 21 cm

    242.5 SPANDREL WITH SPROUTING VINE
       Ink and graphite on laid paper
       28 × 18.5 cm

    242.6 SPANDREL WITH SPROUTING VINE
       Graphite on laid paper
       33.5 × 20.5 cm

    242.7 SPANDREL WITH VINE DECORATION
       Graphite on laid paper
       20 × 17 cm

    242.8 ELEVATION IN NEOCLASSICAL STYLE
       Ink and graphite on laid paper
       7.5 × 21.5 cm

    242.9 SPANDREL WITH FLOWERING VINE
       Ink and graphite on laid paper
       21 × 17.5 cm

    242.10 STUDIES FOR GOTHIC INTERIOR
       Graphite on laid paper
       34.5 × 20.5 cm

244 HOUSE FOR CLEMENT(?)
   LETOURNEAU, PHILADELPHIA (?)
   Theodore Thierry (?), architect
   American vernacular rowhouse, probably from
   the late 1840s; possibly the Philadelphia house

on North 11th above Nectarine Street,
occupied after 1848 by Clement Letourneau,
Jr., a local tanner

244.1 FRONT ELEVATION AND GROUND
PLAN
Ink, graphite, and watercolor on wove paper
50 × 42 cm
Explanatory label in German

246 TOPOGRAPHICAL SURVEY MAPS
Three sheets from a series of maps of an
unidentified river, probably in the United
States

246.1 TURKEY ISLAND, BRIMSTONE
ISLAND, CARSON'S ROCK
Etching on wove paper
22 × 35 cm
Figures numbered 7 and 8

246.2 FLOATING MILL ISLAND, SIMPSONS
ISLAND
Etching on wove paper
21.5 × 35.5 cm
Figures numbered 9 and 10

246.3 HOLEMANS ISLAND, SAND SHOALS
Etching on wove paper
21.5 × 35 cm
Figures numbered 13, 14, and 15

Bibliography

Architectural Association, London. 1982. *Friedrich Wein-brenner, 1766–1826.* London: Architectural Association.

Bentmann, Friedrich. 1969. *Karlsruhe im Blickfeld der Literatur.* Karlsruhe: Badenia.

Berendt, Otto, ed. 1926. *Karlsruhe: Das Buch der Stadt.* Stuttgart: Glaser und Sulz.

Ehrenberg, Kurt. 1908. *Baugeschichte von Karlsruhe, 1715–1820; Bau- und Bodenpolitik: Eine Studie zur Ge-schichte des Städtebaues.* Karlsruhe: Gottlieb Braun.

Everke, Gerhard. 1981. "Weinbrenner—Ein Architect des Klassizismus in der Nachfolge Palladios?" In *Palladio 1508–1580: Architektur der Renaissance—Vorbild für Wein-brenner?* pp. 44–64. Karlsruhe: Städtische Galerie im Prinz-Max-Palais.

Fecht, Karl Gustav. 1887–88. *Geschichte der Haupt- und Residenzstadt Karlsruhe.* 10 fasc. Karlsruhe: Macklot. Re-print. Karlsruhe: Antiquariat der Braunschen Universitätsbuchhandlung, 1976.

Gall, Lothar. 1968. *Der Liberalismus als regierende Partei: Das Grossherzogtum Baden zwischen Restauration und Reichsgründung.* Wiesbaden: Franz Steiner.

Geier, Heinrich. n.d. Student sketchbook of Weinbrenner works. Max Läuger collection.

Goldschmit, Robert. [1915]. *Die Stadt Karlsruhe, ihre Geschichte und ihre Verwaltung: Festschrift zur Erinnerung an das 200 jährige Bestehen der Stadt.* Karlsruhe: C. F. Müller.

Gutman, Emil. 1911. *Das grossherzogliche Residenzschloss zu Karlsruhe.* Heidelberg: Carl Winter. Rev. ed. *Zeitschrift für Geschichte der Architektur,* Beiheft 5, 1911. Reprint. Nedeln, Liechtenstein: Kraus, 1978.

Hammer-Shenk, Harold. 1981. *Synagogen in Deutschland: Geschichte einer Baugattung im 19. und 20. Jahrhundert (1780–1933).* 2 vols. Hamburg: Hans Christian.

Hirsch, Fritz. 1906. *Das bruchsaler Schloss im XIX. Jahrhun-dert.* Heidelberg: Carl Winter.

———. 1928–32. *Hundert Jahre Bauen und Schauen.* 20 fasc. Karlsruhe: Badenia.

Hirschfeld, Peter. 1963. *Die Kunstdenkmäler des Landkreises Rastatt (Ohne Stadt Rastatt und Schloss Favorite).* (Kunst-denkmäler Badens, 12.1) Karlsruhe: C. F. Müller.

Huber, Walter. 1954. *Die Stephanienstrasse: Ein Stück Bau- und Kulturgeschichte aus Karlsruhe.* Karlsruhe: Gottlieb Braun.

Kircher, Gerda. 1959. *Das karlsruher Schloss als Residenz und Musensitz, bearbeitet aus dem Schlossinventar von 1787 und aus der Korrespondenz der Markgräfin Karoline Luise.* Stuttgart: Kohlhammer.

Koebel, Max. [1920]. *Friedrich Weinbrenner.* Berlin: Ernst Wasmuth.

Kolb, Johann Baptist von. 1813–16. *Historisch-statistisch-topographisches Lexicon von dem Grossherzogthum Baden.* 3 vols. Karlsruhe: Gottlieb Braun.

Lacroix, Emil. 1934. "Zur Baugeschichte des karlsruher Marktplatzes: Ein Beitrag zur Geschichte des Städtebaus im 19. Jahrhundert." *Zeitschrift für die Geschichte des Oberrheins* n.s. 47: 24–57.

Lacroix, Emil, Peter Hirschfeld, and Heinrich Niester. 1942. *Die Kunstdenkmäler der Stadt Baden-Baden.* (Kunst-denkmäler Badens, 11.1) Karlsruhe: C. F. Müller.

Lankheit, Klaus. 1976. "Friedrich Weinbrenner—Beiträge zu seinem Werk." *Fridericiana* 19: 5–50.

———. 1979. *Friedrich Weinbrenner und der Denkmalskult um 1800.* Basel and Stuttgart: Birkhäuser.

Lee, Lloyd E. 1980. *The Politics of Harmony: Civil Service, Liberalism, and Social Reform in Baden, 1800–1850.* New-ark: University of Delaware Press.

Liebel, Helen P. 1965. "Enlightened Bureaucracy versus

Enlightened Despotism in Baden, 1750–1792." *Transactions of the American Philosophical Society* 55: 1–132.

Markgräflich Badische Museen, Baden-Baden. 1981. *Carl Friedrich und seine Zeit.* Karlsruhe: C. F. Müller.

Die Residenzstadt Karlsruhe. Ihre Geschichte und Beschreibung; Festgabe der Stadt zur 34. Versammlung deutscher Naturforscher und Aertze. 1858. Karlsruhe: C. F. Müller.

Rott, Hans. 1913. *Die Kunstdenkmäler des Amtsbezirks Bruchsal.* (Kunstdenkmäler des Grossherzogtums Baden, 9.2) Tübingen: J.C.B. Mohr (Paul Siebeck).

Sammlung von Grundplänen, entworfen durch Friedrich Weinbrenner, herausgegeben von mehreren seiner Schüler. 1847–58. 4 fasc. Frankfurt am Main: S. Schmerber.

Schefold, Max. 1971. *Alte Ansichten aus Baden.* 2 vols. Weissenhorn: Anton H. Konrad.

Schirmer, Wulf, Joachim Göricke, et al. 1975. "150 Jahre Universität Karlsruhe, 1825–1975; Architekten der Fridericiana: Skizzen und Entwürfe seit Friedrich Weinbrenner." *Fridericiana* 18.

Schirmer, Wulf. 1977. "Friedrich Weinbrenner, 1766–1826." *Dortmunder Architekturhefte* 4: 117–69.

Schneider, Arthur von. 1961. "Friedrich Weinbrenners Zeichnungen nach antiken Skulpturen." *Miscellanea Bibliothecae Hertzianae* 16: 478–85.

Schumacher, D. c. 1850. "Weinbrenners Wercke gesammelt von D. Schumacher." Album of drawings by students. Landesdenkmalamt, Karlsruhe.

Sinos, Stefan. 1971. "Entwurfsgrundlagen im Werk Friedrich Weinbrenners." *Jahrbuch der staatlichen Kunstsammlungen in Baden-Württemberg* 13: 195–216.

———. 1981. "Friedrich Weinbrenner—Sein Beitrag zur Baukunst des 19. Jahrhunderts." *Karlsruher Beiträge* n.s. 1: 7–59.

Staatliche Kunsthalle, Karlsruhe. 1977. *Friedrich Weinbrenner, 1766–1826: Eine Ausstellung des Instituts für Baugeschichte an der Universität Karlsruhe.* Karlsruhe: G. Braun. Reprint. Karlsruhe: C. F. Müller, 1982.

———. 1978. *Die deutschen Zeichnungen des 19. Jahrhunderts.* 2 vols. Rudolf Theilmann and Edith Ammann, comp. Karlsruhe: Kommissionverlag Müller.

Städtische Galerie im Prinz-Max-Palais, Karlsruhe. 1983. *Heinrich Hübsch, 1795–1863: Der grosse badische Baumeister der Romantik. Ausstellung des Stadtarchivs Karlsruhe und des Instituts für Baugeschichte der Universität Karlsruhe.* Karlsruhe: C. F. Müller.

Stiefel, Karl. 1977. *Baden, 1648–1952.* 2 vols. Karlsruhe: Verein für Oberrheinische Rechts- und Verwaltungsgeschichte. 2d ed. Karlsruhe: Verein für Oberrheinische Rechts- und Verwaltungsgeschichte, 1979.

Stratmann, Rosemarie. 1976. *Schloss Karlsruhe.* Munich: Deutscher Kunstverlag. 2d ed. Munich and Berlin: Deutscher Kunstverlag, 1982.

———. 1980. "Wohnen und Leben im karlsruher Schloss: Über die Repräsentationsräume, insbesondere den Thronsaal, sowie die wechselnde Lage der Wohnquartiere und deren jeweilige Ausstattung." *Zeitschrift für die Geschichte des Oberrheins* 128: 267–91.

Tschira, Arnold. 1939. *Orangerien und Gewächshäuser: Ihre geschichtliche Entwicklung in Deutschland.* Berlin: Deutscher Kunstverlag.

———. 1959. "Der sogenannte Tulla-Plan zur Vergrösserung der Stadt Karlsruhe." *Werke und Wege: Eine Festschrift für Dr. Eberhard Knittel zum 60. Geburtstag,* pp. 31–45. Karlsruhe: Gottlieb Braun.

Valdenaire, Arthur. 1914. *Friedrich Weinbrenner: Seine künstlerische Erziehung und der Ausbau Karlsruhes.* Karlsruhe: C. F. Müller.

———. 1919. *Friedrich Weinbrenner: Sein Leben und seine Bauten.* Karlsruhe: C. F. Müller. 2d ed. Karlsruhe: C. F. Müller, 1926. Reprint. Karlsruhe: C. F. Müller, [1976].

———. 1929. *Karlsruhe: Die klassisch gebaute Stadt.* Augsburg: B. Filser.

———. 1931. *Das karlsruher Schloss.* Karlsruhe: C. F. Müller.

———. 1948. "Die karlsruher Marktplatz." *Zeitschrift für die Geschichte des Oberrheins* n.s. 57: 415–49.

Weech, Friedrich Otto Aristides von. 1890. *Badische Geschichte.* Karlsruhe: A. Bielefeld. Reprint. Magstadt bei Stuttgart: Horst Bissinger, 1981.

Weinbrenner, Friedrich. 1810–25. *Architektonisches Lehrbuch.* 3 vols. Tübingen: J. G. Cotta. Karlsruhe: D. R. Marx.

———. 1814. *Ideen zu einem teutschen Nationaldenkmal des entscheidenden Sieges bey Leipzig, mit Grund und Auf-Rissen.* Karlsruhe: D. R. Marx.

———. 1818. *Vorschlag zu einem Sieges-Denkmal für das Schlachtfeld bei Belle-Alliance.* Leipzig: Georg Voss. 2d ed. Karlsruhe: D. R. Marx, 1820.

———. 1822–35. *Ausgeführte und projectirte Gebäude.* Vols. 1, 2, 3, 7 (vols. 4–6 never published). Karlsruhe and Baden-Baden: D. R. Marx. Reprint with Kommentar by Wulf Schirmer. Karlsruhe: C. F. Müller, 1978.

——. 1822–34. *Entwurfe und Ergänzungen antiker Gebäude.* 2 vols. Karlsruhe and Baden-Baden: D. R. Marx.

——. 1926. *Briefe und Aufsätze.* Arthur Valdenaire, ed. Karlsruhe: Gottlieb Braun.

——. 1958. *Denkwürdigkeiten.* Arthur von Schneider, ed. Karlsruhe: Gottlieb Braun.

Weller, Arnold. 1979. *Sozialgeschichte Südwestdeutschlands: Unter besonderer Berücksichtigung der sozialen und karitativen Arbeit vom späten Mittelalter bis zur Gegenwart.* Stuttgart: Konrad Theiss.

Concordance of Inventory Numbers

OLD	NEW	OLD	NEW	OLD	NEW
no no. & A146	6.5	A36	58.4	A69	76.1
002	108.1	A37	14.2	A70	2.3
A4	70.1	A38	14.1	A71	84.1
A5	146.1	A39	58.3	A72 & A73	98.1
A6	48.2	A40	58.2	A73 & A72	98.1
A7 & A8	82.1	A41	58.1	A74	124.1
A8 & A7	82.1	A42	106.1	A75	200.1
A9	56.5	A43	92.1	A76	100.1
A10	4.1	A44	92.2	A77	182.1
A11	144.1	A45	92.3	A78 & A80	6.4
A12	144.2	A46	120.1	A79	6.1
A13	164.1	A47	122.1	A80 & A78	6.4
A14	154.1	A48	118.1	A81	2.15
A15	66.1	A49	170.1	A82	12.1
A16	72.1	A51	178.1	A83	6.3
A17	146.2	A52	6.2	A84	2.12
A18	56.4	A53	30.3	A85	38.1
A21	150.1	A54	30.2	A86	64.1
A22	150.2	A55	120.2	A87	88.2
A23	54.2	A55.1	116.1	A88	88.1
A25	56.3	A56	134.1	A89	6.6
A25a	210.20	A57	46.1	A90	110.1
A26	56.2	A58	136.1	A91	194.9
A27	94.2	A59	2.13	A92	194.13
A28	94.1	A60	90.4	A93	152.2
A28a	210.6	A61	198.6	A94	194.12
A29	54.1	A62	80.1	A95	194.11
A30	176.1	A63	50.1	A96	156.1
A31	194.15	A64	240.1	A97	194.10
A32	60.1	A65	48.1	A98	194.8
A33	148.1	A66	28.1	A99	194.14
A34	58.6	A67	180.1	A100	112.1
A35	58.5	A68	68.1	A101	110.2

OLD	NEW	OLD	NEW	OLD	NEW
A102	152.1	A147	8.1	A199	2.16
A103	126.1	A148	30.1	A200	18.2
A104	160.1	A149	128.1	A201	212.1
A105	158.1	A150	104.1	A202	226.4
A106	74.1	A151	20.1	A203	194.2
A107	174.1	A152	26.1	A204	246.3
A108	78.1	A153	32.1	A205	246.2
A109	114.1	A154	4.4	A207	226.14
A110	2.4	A155	4.2	A208	226.16
A111	2.7	A156	96.3	A209	204.1
A112 & A115	2.1	A157	96.1	A210	188.1
A113	2.6	A158	96.2	A211	194.7
A114	2.2	A159	4.5	A212	184.1
A115 & A112	2.1	A160	4.3	A213	194.6
A116	2.5	A161	130.1	A214	194.1
A117	114.2	A162	132.1	A215	194.3
A119	102.1	A163	24.1	A216	194.4
A120	16.1	A168	244.1	A217	52.1
A121	166.1	A170	36.1	A218	86.1
A122	16.2	A171	198.1	A219	34.1
A123	10.1	A172	192.1	A220	218.2
A124	56.1	A173	198.2	A221	220.1
A125	62.1	A174	226.3	A222	210.1
A126	62.2	A176	228.1	A223	210.11
A127	162.1	A177	194.5	A224	218.8
A128	162.5	A178	2.14	A225	226.17
A129	162.4	A179	44.1	A226	234.1
A130	162.3	A180	44.2	A227	218.9
A131	162.2	A181	40.1	A228	226.12
A132	162.6	A182	226.2	A229	210.23
A133	108.2	A185	198.3	A230	226.1
A134	108.3	A186	208.1	A231	242.9
A135	2.11	A187	196.2	A232	242.5
A136	2.9	A188	196.1	A233	210.18
A137	2.10	A189	246.1	A234	238.1
A138	2.8	A192	230.1	A235	242.7
A139	172.1	A194	198.5	A236	242.4
A140 & A141	20.2	A195	168.1	A237	210.26
A141 & A140	20.2	A196 [top]	42.3	A238	210.14
A142	90.2	A196 [bottom]	42.4	A239	242.2
A143	90.1	A197 [top]	42.1	A240	220.2
A144	90.3	A197 [bottom]	42.2	A241	210.15
A145	18.1	A198 [top]	42.5	A242	216.1
A146 & no no.	6.5	A198 [bottom]	42.6	A243	226.19

OLD	NEW	OLD	NEW	OLD	NEW
A245	218.4	A267	242.1	A286	218.10
A246	218.5	A268	226.11	A287	226.15
A247	218.6	A269	210.16	A288	186.1
A248	218.7	A270	218.3	A289	190.1
A249	210.21	A271	210.28	A290	210.13
A250	210.10	A272	226.20	A291	242.8
A251	210.17	A273	210.22	A292	232.1
A252	226.5	A274	210.19	A293	206.1
A253	223.1	A275	210.4	A294	210.12
A255	214.2	A276	226.10	A295	236.1
A256	214.1	A277	210.5	A296	210.3
A257	218.1	A278	210.25	A297	218.11
A258	242.3	A279	210.24	A298	210.8
A259	226.6	A280	226.8	A299	210.7
A261	242.6	A280 [sic]	226.13	A299 [sic]	206.1
A262	242.10	A281	226.18	A300	198.4
A263	210.9	A282	210.27	A301	224.1
A264	226.9	A283	226.7	A302	202.1
A265	221.1	A285	210.2	A303	210.29